THE COUNTERTERROR COALITIONS

Cooperation with Europe, NATO, and the European Union

Nora Bensahel

Prepared for the United States Air Force
Approved for public release; distribution unlimited

RAND Project AIR FORCE

The research reported here was sponsored by the United States Air Force under Contract F49642-01-C-0003. Further information may be obtained from the Strategic Planning Division, Directorate of Plans, Hq USAF.

Library of Congress Cataloging-in-Publication Data

Bensahel, Nora, 1971–
    The counterterror coalitions : cooperation with Europe, NATO, and the European Union / Nora Bensahel.
      p. cm.
    "MR-1746."
    Includes bibliographical references.
    ISBN 0-8330-3444-8 (pbk.)
    1. United States—Military policy. 2. United States—Military relations—Europe. 3. Europe—Military relations—United States. 4. Terrorism—Prevention. 5. War on Terrorism, 2001– 6. North Atlantic Treaty Organization. 7. European Union. I.Title.

UA23.B39995 2003
363.32—dc22

                                  2003014991

Published 2003 by RAND
1700 Main Street, P.O. Box 2138, Santa Monica, CA 90407-2138
1200 South Hayes Street, Arlington, VA 22202-5050
201 North Craig Street, Suite 202, Pittsburgh, PA 15213-1516
RAND URL: http://www.rand.org/
To order RAND documents or to obtain additional information, contact Distribution Services: Telephone: (310) 451-7002;
Fax: (310) 451-6915; Email: order@rand.org

Shortly after the September 11 attacks, Air Force Chief of Staff General John Jumper asked RAND to conduct a study entitled "Thinking Strategically About Combating Terrorism." This year-long project was divided into four research tasks, each tackling different but complementary aspects of the counterterrorism problem:

- Threat assessment: identifying the character and boundaries of the threat

- The international dimension: assessing the impact of coalition and other international actors on U.S. options

- Strategy: designing an overarching counterterror strategy

- Implications for the Air Force: identifying promising applications of air and space power.

The research for this report was conducted as part of the second task, on international aspects of counterterror cooperation. It examines European responses to the September 11 attacks and the subsequent war in Afghanistan, and assesses the types of cooperation that the United States will need from Europe to achieve its counterterror objectives. It also assesses the ways in which NATO and the European Union are reforming their agendas to address the threat of terrorism and the areas of mutual cooperation that will most benefit the United States.

This report is part of a series on international counterterror cooperation. Forthcoming reports in this series will examine other regions of the world, including the former Soviet Union and South

Asia, and will assess the linkages between different functional areas of international cooperation against terrorism. Although these reports address a wide variety of subjects, they build on a common principle: counterterror cooperation occurs across numerous issue areas, including military, financial, law enforcement, and intelligence. An effective counterterror strategy will need to address each of these dimensions and account for some of the synergies and frictions among them.

Publications to date from the other three project tasks include:

- Lynn Davis, Steve Hosmer, Sara Daly, and Karl Mueller, *The U.S. Counterterrorism Strategy: A Planning Framework to Facilitate Timely Adjustments*, DB-426-AF

- David Ochmanek, *Military Operations Against Terrorist Groups Abroad: Implications for the U.S. Air Force*, MR-1738-AF.

The research for this report was sponsored by General John Jumper, Chief of Staff of the United States Air Force. The study, conducted as part of the Strategy and Doctrine Program of RAND's Project AIR FORCE, is examining a wide range of strategic responses to the evolving terrorist threat. Comments are welcome and may be addressed to the author or to the Program Director, Dr. Edward Harshberger.

Research for this report was completed in early 2003.

PROJECT AIR FORCE

Project AIR FORCE (PAF) a division of RAND, is the U.S. Air Force's federally funded research and development center for studies and analyses. PAF provides the Air Force with independent analyses of policy alternatives affecting the development, employment, combat readiness, and support of current and future aerospace forces. Research is performed in four programs: Aerospace Force Development; Manpower, Personnel, and Training; Resource Management; and Strategy and Doctrine.

Additional information about PAF is available on our web site at http://www.rand.org/paf.

CONTENTS

TABLE

The September 11, 2001 terrorist attacks against the World Trade Center and the Pentagon were widely interpreted in Europe as a broader attack on Western values of freedom, tolerance, and openness. Leaders from states throughout the continent pledged their willingness to cooperate in counterterror efforts. NATO invoked its Article 5 collective defense provision for the first time in its history, and other European organizations also expressed their support.

Although Operation Enduring Freedom in Afghanistan started off with few openly acknowledged coalition contributions, coalition forces became increasingly acknowledged and important as the operation continued. European countries provided a wide range of capabilities on a bilateral basis, including special forces, air forces, naval forces, ground forces, and specialized units. The United States accepted only a few contributions from NATO as an organization, and many alliance members were dissatisfied with the small role given to the alliance after its dramatic invocation of Article 5. Questions over NATO's proper role and mission became increasingly intense as transatlantic tensions over Iraq grew, revealing some fundamental divisions between the United States and the Europeans as well as among the Europeans themselves (see pp. 17–22).

The long-term success of the counterterror campaign will depend on concerted cooperation from European states, but a key question (addressed in Chapter Three) is the extent to which that cooperation should be pursued through European multilateral institutions. NATO has not yet proven capable of reorienting itself to challenge terrorism. It has adopted a number of initiatives to improve its counterterror capabilities, including a military concept for combating terrorism and a NATO Response Force, but progress remains limited by the fact that the allies still disagree about whether countering terrorism should become one of NATO's primary missions. The European Union (EU) is limited in its military and intelligence capabilities, but it has undertaken a number of important initiatives in Justice and Home Affairs. Measures such as adopting a common European arrest warrant, strengthening Europol, and harmonizing policies on money laundering and other financial crimes may prove extremely valuable for counterterrorism efforts.

As the United States develops a policy of counterterror cooperation with Europe, it must strike the right balance between bilateral and multilateral approaches. The policy choice is not *whether* to pursue bilateral or multilateral approaches; many important policies are now being made at the European level and multilateral institutions cannot simply be ignored. Instead, the United States must determine *which issues* are best addressed through a multilateral approach and which ones are best addressed through a bilateral approach.

This report argues that the United States should pursue military and intelligence cooperation on a bilateral basis, and it should increasingly pursue financial and law enforcement cooperation on a multilateral basis. (See pp. 45–54.) Bilateral cooperation will remain necessary in the military and intelligence realms—states retain significant capacities in these areas, NATO currently lacks the political will to embrace counterterrorism as a new mission, and the EU does not intend to build the centralized structures and offensive capabilities that would be required. By contrast, the EU has made extraordinary progress in the financial and law enforcement aspects of counterterrorism in recent years. Although individual states have important capabilities in these areas that must be utilized, the United States should adopt an increasingly multilateral approach as EU cooperation progresses. The EU still has a long way to go before it achieves robust multilateral capabilities in the financial and law enforcement areas, yet it is uniquely positioned to coordinate its members' efforts, to analyze data, and to identify emerging trends throughout the continent. Multilateral cooperation with an increasingly strong EU will enhance the ability of states on both sides of the Atlantic to prevent terrorism and to prosecute those involved in terrorist activities.

ACKNOWLEDGMENTS

Many individuals assisted with the research for this report. First, the author wishes to thank Olga Oliker for her involvement and excellent advice through all stages of the research. Ted Harshberger provided guidance and suggestions throughout the project, as well as during some of the research trips.

At United States European Command, the author and the rest of the research team are grateful to Major General Jeffrey Kohler (USAF), Director, Plans and Policy, for sponsoring our visit, and to LTC John Frame (USA) and CPT Jeffrey Sargent (USA) for arranging our meetings. We thank the various officers and civilians we met with from ECJ2, ECJ3, ECJ4, ECJ5, SOCEUR, the Joint Planning Group, the Joint Interagency Coordination Group, and the Political Advisor's office.

At United States Air Forces Europe, Brigadier General Mark Welsh sponsored our visit, and Michael McMullen arranged a detailed set of meetings for us. We thank the many officers from A2, A3, A5, DO, LGX, UTASC, and XP who spent time with us.

At NATO, we thank Diane Zeleny and Judith Windsor-Ritzolati, United States Information Office, Office of Information and Press, for arranging our meetings. On the NATO staff, we thank Dr. Edgar Buckley, Assistant Secretary General for Defense Planning and Operations; Steve Orosz, Director of Civil Emergency Planning; Colonel Jonathan Parish (British Army), Plans and Policy Division, International Military Staff; Steven Sturm, Defense Planning and Policy Division; Ted Whiteside, Director of the Weapons of Mass Destruction Office; and Damon Wilson, Office of the Secretary General. We also thank Nigel Brind, U.K. Mission to NATO; François-

Xavier Carrel-Billard, French Mission to NATO; and Lt Col Inge Gedo, Joe Manso, and Col Thomas Rendall, U.S. Mission to NATO.

At the European Union, we thank Dierdrick Paalman, Directorate General for Justice and Home Affairs, European Commission; Fraser Cameron and Yves Mollard la Bruyère, Directorate General for External Relations, European Commission; and Oliver Nette, Delegation of the European Union to the United States.

We also thank John Lellenberg, Scott Schless, and Alisa Stack-O'Connor, U.S. Department of Defense; Marc Richard, U.S. Department of Justice; Maren Brooks and Jim Wagner, U.S. Department of State; Colonel Anne Moisan (USAF), National Defense University; and John Occhipinti, Canisius College.

At RAND, John E. Peters and Michael Spirtas provided careful and thoughtful reviews of earlier drafts that greatly improved the final report. Risha Henneman and Miriam Schafer provided invaluable administrative assistance.

AWACS	Airborne Warning and Control System
CFSP	Common Foreign and Security Policy
DCI	Defense Capabilities Initiative
DPC	Defense Planning Committee
ECOFIN	Council of Economic and Finance Ministers
ESDP	European Security and Defense Policy
EU	European Union
ISAF	International Security Assistance Force
JHA	Justice and Home Affairs
MLAT	mutual legal assistance treaty
NAC	North Atlantic Council
NATO	North Atlantic Treaty Organization
NBC	nuclear, biological, and chemical
NRF	NATO Response Force
OEF	Operation Enduring Freedom (Afghanistan)
OPTEMPO	operational tempo
PCC	Prague Capabilities Commitment
PfP	Partnership for Peace
SACEUR	Supreme Allied Commander, Europe

SACLANT	Supreme Allied Commander, Atlantic
UN	United Nations
WMD	weapons of mass destruction

Chapter One

INTRODUCTION

The Europeans have been, and are likely to continue to be, the United States' closest partners in the counterterror campaign. The September 11, 2001 terrorist attacks against the World Trade Center and the Pentagon were widely interpreted in Europe as a broader attack on Western values of freedom, tolerance, and openness. Memorial services and candlelight vigils erupted almost spontaneously in many European cities, expressing the sentiment captured in the now-famous French newspaper headline, "We are all Americans."[1]

Leaders from states throughout western and eastern Europe immediately expressed their support for the United States after the attacks and pledged to cooperate in counterterror efforts. The North Atlantic Treaty Organization (NATO) unanimously condemned the attacks within hours of their occurrence, and on September 12 it took the unprecedented step of invoking NATO's collective defense provisions for the first time in its 52-year history. The European Union (EU) also declared its solidarity with the United States on the day after the attacks, and its members pledged both their individual and their collective support for any counterterrorism efforts.

In the following months, the Europeans worked closely with the United States to address the terrorist problem. The Europeans have staunchly supported the United States in their diplomatic statements, have worked with the United States and the United Nations

---

[1]Jean-Marie Colombani, "Nous sommes tous Américains," *Le Monde*, September 12, 2001.

to disrupt sources of terrorist financing, and have increased law enforcement and intelligence cooperation with the United States to make it more difficult for terrorists to move freely both within and across national borders. Many European countries contributed military forces to Operation Enduring Freedom, which ousted the Taliban from power in Afghanistan, and are currently contributing the personnel, commanders, and headquarters structures for the International Security Assistance Force (ISAF) that is charged with maintaining stability in and around Kabul. European contributions to these operations are perhaps the most visible in the military area, but they should not obscure significant cooperation in other areas as well.

The Europeans have provided much of this support through multilateral channels. During the past decade, European institutions have grown and evolved in ways that are changing the landscape of Europe. NATO, once an organization designed to counter the threat of a Soviet invasion, has expanded to include former adversaries in central and eastern Europe and has adopted new strategic concepts that enable the alliance to counter threats to its members' interests anywhere around the world. The European Union achieved a common internal market, introduced a common currency, expanded its competency to new areas, and is slowly developing a common foreign and security policy. Individual European states are becoming ever more enmeshed in a web of institutional arrangements that affect their domestic and foreign policies—and European states that do not yet belong to these institutions are desperately trying to join them.

These developments mean that the United States will need to adopt an increasingly multilateral approach in some aspects of counterterror cooperation. The United States has traditionally preferred bilateral diplomacy, because it is much easier to interact with a single state rather than a multilateral institution. A bilateral approach also allows the United States to exploit differences in European policy preferences by securing support from countries that agree with it before the European Union can seek the compromises necessary to reach a common EU position. Yet the strengthening of the European Union, particularly in Justice and Home Affairs, makes this process more challenging. In law enforcement and countering terrorist financing, the United States may find an increasing need to engage and negotiate with the EU as a whole rather than with its individual members. Yet neither NATO nor the EU has yet developed the multilateral capabilities necessary for military and intelligence counterterror cooperation. For the foreseeable future, the United States will need to rely on bilateral cooperation in these two important areas.

Chapter Two of this report examines European responses to September 11, both bilaterally and within NATO, and European participation in the war in Afghanistan. Chapter Three analyzes the extent to which NATO and the European Union are adapting to the challenges of the counterterrorism campaign and identifies how the events of September 11 have changed the agendas of both organizations. Chapter Four concludes by arguing that the United States may best be served by pursuing bilateral approaches in the military and intelligence aspects of counterterror cooperation, while pursuing an increasingly multilateral approach in the law enforcement and financial areas.

Chapter Two

SEPTEMBER 11 AND THE WAR ON TERRORISM

The European countries were extremely supportive of the United States after September 11. They pledged to support the United States individually, in personal conversations with President Bush and senior U.S. policymakers, and collectively, through NATO and the European Union. NATO's invocation of its self-defense clause led many to expect that NATO would be an integral part of the military response in Afghanistan, in that the alliance was built around the principle that an attack on one member would be considered an attack on all. Yet it soon became clear that the United States would conduct military operations in Afghanistan without any explicit NATO role, preferring instead to incorporate European contributions on a bilateral basis.

NATO AND THE ARTICLE 5 DECLARATION

NATO reacted swiftly and strongly to the September 11 attacks. Within hours, the North Atlantic Council (NAC) unanimously condemned the attacks and pledged its assistance and support.[1] NATO Secretary General Lord Robertson, speaking with Secretary of State Colin Powell later that evening, encouraged the United States to formally invoke the collective self-defense provisions included in Article 5 of the NATO Charter. Robertson later recalled that he told Powell that "invoking Article 5 would be a useful statement of political backing, that it would help the United States build an instant anti-

---

[1]"Statement by the North Atlantic Council," Press Release PR/CP (2001)122, September 11, 2001.

terror coalition based in part on the moral authority behind Article 5, and that it would be a deterrent—in that whoever was responsible for the attack would know they had taken on not just the United States, but also the greatest military alliance in the world."[2]   U.S. officials soon responded that they would welcome an invocation of Article 5, even though they later stressed that they had not officially asked NATO to do so.[3]

Robertson quickly set out to build a consensus among NATO's 19 members. Some of the allies expressed reservations about invoking Article 5, including Germany, Belgium, and Norway, and objections from the Netherlands delayed the final decision for several hours.[4] Yet Robertson strongly pushed the allies toward consensus, arguing that failing to invoke Article 5 in response to such blatant attacks would fundamentally weaken the alliance and undermine its ability to respond to future crises. At 9:30 pm on September 12, NATO invoked Article 5 for the first time in its 52-year history. The North Atlantic Council issued a statement that read in part:

> The Council agreed that if it is determined that this attack was directed from abroad against the United States, it shall be regarded as an action covered by Article 5 of the Washington Treaty, which states that an armed attack against one or more of the Allies in Europe or North America shall be considered an attack against them all.[5]

Senior U.S. officials held a series of classified briefings for the NATO members during the next several weeks, presenting evidence that al Qaeda had planned and executed the attacks. On October 2, NATO officially reached agreement that the attacks had originated abroad,

---

[2]James Kitfield, "NATO Metamorphosis," *National Journal*, Vol. 34, No. 6, February 9, 2002, pp. 376–380.

[3]Suzanne Daley, "For First Time, NATO Invokes Pact with U.S.," *New York Times*, September 13, 2001; interviews with NATO civilian officials, July 2002.

[4]Joseph Fitchett, "NATO Unity, But What Next?" *International Herald Tribune*, September 14, 2001.

[5]"Statement by the North Atlantic Council," Press Release (2001)124, September 12, 2001.

and that they would therefore be considered an action covered by Article 5.[6]

Many NATO members hoped that invoking Article 5 would lead the United States to conduct any military response against al Qaeda under the NATO flag, or at least coordinate its actions with the integrated military structure and political institutions. Yet by early October, the U.S. decisionmakers made clear that the alliance would not be involved in any military actions against Afghanistan. As one U.S. senior official noted, "I think it's safe to say that we won't be asking SACEUR [the Supreme Allied Commander, Europe] to put together a battle plan for Afghanistan."[7] The United States did ask NATO to provide certain forms of support, however. On October 3, the United States asked NATO to provide assistance in eight specific areas:

- Enhance intelligence sharing and cooperation

- Assist states facing an increased terrorist threat as a result of supporting the campaign against terrorism

- Increase security at U.S. and allied facilities on NATO territory

- Backfill selected allied assets in NATO's area of responsibility that redeploy to support counterterror operations

- Provide blanket overflight clearances for the United States and other allies for operations against terrorism

- Provide port and airfield access for the United States and other allies for operations against terrorism

- Deploy elements of NATO's standing naval forces to the Mediterranean, if requested

---

[6]The U.S. policymakers who briefed NATO included Deputy Secretary of State Richard Armitage, Deputy Secretary of Defense Paul Wolfowitz, and the State Department Coordinator for Counterterrorism Frank Taylor. "Statement by NATO Secretary General, Lord Robertson," October 2, 2001.

[7]Philip H. Gordon, "NATO After 11 September," *Survival*, Vol. 43, No. 4, Winter 2001–2002, p. 92.

- Deploy elements of the NATO Early Warning Force for operations against terrorism, if requested.[8]

The NAC unanimously approved all eight measures, and the allies announced that they were prepared, both individually and collectively within NATO, to support the United States. These measures all facilitated U.S. military planning efforts, especially the provisions for blanket overflight rights and port and airfield access, and allowed the United States to consider redeploying any forces involved in ongoing NATO operations.[9] Many of the aspiring NATO countries also agreed to provide these forms of support, which meant that U.S. planners could prepare to use airspace, ports, and airfields through most of western and eastern Europe without having to negotiate bilateral agreements with each individual state.[10]

NATO did not contribute any of its collective assets to Operation Enduring Freedom in Afghanistan, although it did deploy naval forces to the Mediterranean as a signal of solidarity and resolve. The NAC did direct the alliance to develop contingency plans for humanitarian assistance missions in Afghanistan, but those efforts never went beyond the planning stage.[11]

NATO did, however, play an important role in Operation Noble Eagle, the homeland security operation in the United States. Five NATO Airborne Warning and Control System (AWACS) aircraft, part of the NATO Early Warning Force, started patrolling the United States in October, in an operation that became known as Eagle Assist. These NATO surveillance aircraft, which have multinational crews, were deployed to the United States in order to allow U.S.

---

[8]"Statement to the Press by NATO Secretary General, Lord Robertson, on the North Atlantic Council Decision on Implementation of Article 5 of the Washington Treaty Following the 11 September Attacks Against the United States," October 4, 2001.

[9]Tom Lansford, *All for One: Terrorism, NATO and the United States*, Ashgate, Aldershot, UK, 2002, p. 111.

[10]Lansford, p. 111; interviews with U.S. military officials, July 2002.

[11]The North Atlantic Council authorized this planning on November 13, 2001, shortly before the unexpectedly rapid collapse of the Taliban government. Lansford, p. 138; interviews with NATO officials, July 2002.

AWACS to be redeployed for missions in Afghanistan.[12] These NATO planes flew missions throughout the fall and winter, and in February 2002, NATO deployed two additional AWACS to help provide security during the Winter Olympics in Salt Lake City. In late April, the United States told NATO that the security threat had declined and that the NATO AWACS would no longer be needed. By the time the last NATO AWACS left the United States in May, the aircraft had flown more than 360 missions—a quarter of all the AWACS patrols over the United States during that time—with 830 crew members from 13 alliance countries.[13]

BILATERAL CONTRIBUTIONS TO OPERATION ENDURING FREEDOM

While the European states collectively pledged their support for the United States through NATO, they also offered concrete military support to Operation Enduring Freedom (OEF) on a bilateral basis. The United States received so many offers of military support that policymakers struggled in September and October 2001 to determine the best ways to use them.[14] While the offers were numerous, their operational utility was often questionable. As a result, the United States ended up declining most of the offers of combat forces that it received. In many cases, the United States would have had to deploy and sustain the offered contingents, and U.S. policymakers did not want to overburden U.S. transportation and logistics networks. In other cases, the offered contingents were not appropriate for the military plans being developed, leading some U.S. civilian and military personnel to speculate that the offers were made to gain the po-

---

[12]"Statement by NATO Secretary General, Lord Robertson," Press Release (2001)138, October 8 , 2001.

[13]The 13 countries were Belgium, Canada, Denmark, Germany, Greece, Italy, the Netherlands, Norway, Portugal, Spain, Turkey, the United Kingdom, and the United States. Jack Dorsey, "NATO Air Surveillance Help Makes American Skies Safer," *Norfolk Virginian-Pilot*, October 24, 2001; Gregory Piatt, "NATO's AWACS Leaving Skies Over U.S., Returning to Europe," *Baltimore Sun*, April 25, 2002; Eric Schmitt, "NATO Planes to End Patrols of U.S. Skies," *New York Times*, May 2, 2002.

[14]Interviews with NATO civilian officials, July 2002.

litical benefits of supporting the United States without having to follow through by actually participating in military operations.[15]

However, a few offers of combat forces were accepted, and European militaries figured prominently among the forces that participated in operations in Afghanistan. The United Kingdom and France contributed a wide variety of types of forces to the operations, while most other countries provided smaller contingents, often with specialized capabilities and skills. More important, European countries in both the western and eastern parts of the continent provided crucial basing, access, and overflight rights. Table 2.1 summarizes these contributions, and the full list of European contributions to Operation Enduring Freedom can be found in the appendix.

Table 2.1

Summary of European and Canadian Contributions to Operation Enduring Freedom

Country	Special Forces	Air Forces	Naval Forces	Ground Forces	Other Forces
Canada	X	X	X	X	
Czech Republic					X
Denmark	X	X			
Estonia					X
France	X	X	X	X	
Germany	X	X	X		X
Greece			X	X	
Italy		X	X		
Latvia		X			
The Netherlands		X	X		
Norway	X	X			X
Poland	X		X		X
Portugal		X			X
Romania				X	
Russia					X
Slovakia					X
Spain		X	X		X
Turkey	X	X		X	
United Kingdom	X	X	X	X	X

---

[15]Interviews with U.S. government and military officials, May, June, and July 2002.

Special Forces

Special forces from Denmark, France, Germany, Norway, Turkey, the United Kingdom, and elsewhere played a critical role in Operation Enduring Freedom. Special forces from these countries often operated under U.S. command in a wide variety of missions, which included hunting down fleeing members of al Qaeda and the Taliban, gathering intelligence, and advising the Northern Alliance. The United Kingdom was the first country to openly acknowledge the participation of its special forces, stating on November 11, 2001, that British special forces were offering advice and assistance to the Northern Alliance.[16] Other European countries acknowledged in the spring of 2002 the role of their special forces, which were used extensively in Operation Anaconda (in the mountains of eastern Afghanistan) and the series of raids that followed. These special forces were extraordinarily important to the success of the overall operation, easing some of the burden on U.S. special forces and often offering unique capabilities. U.S. military officers particularly praised the capabilities of the Norwegian special forces, for example, because their extensive mountain training proved useful in Afghanistan's rocky terrain.[17]

Air Forces

Many European countries contributed support aircraft to Operation Enduring Freedom, but France was the only country whose air force jets had participated in strike operations as of this writing.[18] France deployed six Mirage 2000D strike aircraft to Kyrgyzstan in February 2002, and they soon joined French carrier-based aircraft in conduct-

---

[16]The British press reported that members of the SAS, Britain's highly trained and highly regarded special forces, entered Afghanistan within days of the September 11 attacks to prepare for covert operations and to gather intelligence. Michael Evans, "SAS Already Gathering Intelligence in Afghanistan," *The Times* (London), September 21, 2001; Michael Smith, "Hoon Confirms that British Troops Are on the Front Line," *The Daily Telegraph* (London), November 12, 2001.

[17]Interviews with U.S. military officials, June 2002.

[18]Denmark, the Netherlands, and Norway deployed F-16s to the region, but as of December 2002, the aircraft seem to have been used mostly for reconnaissance.

ing offensive strikes during Operation Anaconda.[19] France also contributed two C-135FR tankers, which refueled French and U.S. naval aircraft, as well as C-130 and C-160 transport aircraft.[20]

The United Kingdom provided a large number of support aircraft to operations in Afghanistan, where its tankers made a particularly critical contribution. Because U.S. carrier-based aircraft needed to be refueled twice on their way to Afghanistan, sometimes more, British refueling capabilities relieved some of the burden placed on U.S. refuelers. Two British Tristars and four British VC-10s flew 120 hours every 28 days—four times their peacetime operational tempo (OPTEMPO) rate—and refueled approximately 20 percent of the aircraft used in ground attacks. The Royal Air Force also provided a number of surveillance and reconnaissance aircraft to OEF, including AWACS, E-3D Sentry aircraft, Nimrod R1s and MR2s, and Canberra PR-9s.[21]

Other European countries provided smaller numbers of support aircraft. Denmark, Germany, Italy, the Netherlands, Norway, and Spain all contributed C-130s and other transport aircraft, which took some of the load off of U.S theater airlift assets. Although Bulgaria, the Netherlands, and Turkey provided aerial refuelers, the Bulgarian tanker and the Dutch transport aircraft were authorized by their governments to support humanitarian operations only.

---

[19]"190 French Troops Arrive in Kyrgyzstan to Help with Base," *Los Angeles Times*, February 3, 2002; Philip Shishkin, "Europe Has Chance to Prove Mettle in Current Offensive in Afghanistan," *Wall Street Journal*, March 6, 2002; Jeremy Shapiro, *The Role of France in the War on Terrorism*, Center on the United States and France, Brookings Institution, May 2002.

[20]Embassy of France in the United States, "French Military Contibution [sic] to the Fight Against Terrorism," available at http://www.ambafrance-us.org/news/statmnts/2002/sfia/fight1.asp, accessed October 4, 2002.

[21]"Operation Veritas—British Forces," British Ministry of Defence, available at http://www.operations.mod.uk/veritas/forces.htm, accessed October 2, 2002. For an anecdotal discussion of the relationship between British AWACS aircraft and U.S. fighters, see Mark Bowden, "The Kabul-ki Dance," *The Atlantic Monthly*, November 2002, pp. 66–87.

Naval Forces

European naval forces provided important support for operations in Afghanistan. The United Kingdom deployed the largest British naval task force since the Gulf War in support of the operation, formed around the aircraft carrier HMS *Illustrious* and the assault ship HMS *Fearless*. Three Royal Navy submarines fired Tomahawk missiles against Afghan targets twice during the first week of Operation Enduring Freedom, the only time that coalition naval forces participated in standoff strike operations.[22] France deployed the aircraft carrier *Charles de Gaulle* and its battle group in December 2001, and started flying combat sorties later that month. The 28 fighters in the carrier group conducted 10 percent of all reconnaissance and air defense operations in Afghanistan between the end of December 2001 and mid-March 2002, and the total French naval contribution to OEF involved 24 percent of the entire French navy.[23] Italy also contributed its carrier battle group, later relieved by a destroyer and a frigate, and both Spain and Greece deployed naval assets.[24]

In addition to these combat contributions, several European countries participated in a maritime interception operation off the Horn of Africa. This continuing operation, known as Task Force 150, seeks to prevent al Qaeda and Taliban forces from fleeing to Africa. The United States, Germany, and Spain have all taken turns commanding the task force, which is primarily composed of ships from those three countries. The large German contribution is particularly notable, because it marked the first deployment of German ships to the Middle East in over 50 years.[25] The task force had made more than 15,000 queries of ships in the region and had boarded 184 vessels as

---

[22]"Operation Veritas—British Forces."

[23]J. A. C. Lewis, "French Fighters Join Action in Afghanistan," *Jane's Defence Weekly*, March 13, 2002; Department of Defense Public Affairs Fact Sheet, *International Contributions to the War Against Terrorism*, June 7, 2002 (revised June 14, 2002), available at http://www/defenselink.mil/news/Jun2002/d20020607contributions.pdf, accessed October 4, 2002.

[24]U.S. Central Command, "International Contributions to the War on Terrorism," available at http://www.centcom.mil/Operations/Coalition/joint.htm, accessed November 2002.

[25]U.S. Central Command.

of mid-July 2002.[26] Some observers have argued that this task force lacks the numbers of ships and the authority necessary for its mission, but U.S. military officials consider it a highly important coalition effort.[27] Its most notable operation occurred in December 2002, when two Spanish ships from the task force intercepted a ship operated by a North Korean crew that was transporting disassembled Scud missiles to Yemen.[28]

Land Forces

British Royal Marines were the largest contingent of coalition land forces to participate in Operation Enduring Freedom. Toward the end of October 2001, the British press began reporting that the government was planning to send some 1000 Royal Marines, along with additional special forces and support groups, to conduct ground operations as part of OEF.[29] In late November, it seemed that the British ground contribution could be even larger, when the government put 6400 troops on 48-hour alert for a possible deployment. However, those troops were downgraded to a one-week alert once Kabul fell, and the Taliban collapsed faster than anyone had anticipated.[30] On March 18, 2002, the British government announced that it would send an additional 1700 troops to participate in operations against Taliban and al Qaeda resistance, fulfilling a U.S. request for assistance after the unexpectedly tough fighting during Operation

---

[26]David Brown, "Coalition Aircraft Patrol the Seas for Enduring Freedom," *Navy Times*, August 12, 2002.

[27]Interviews with U.S. military personnel, June 2002.

[28]The United States encouraged the Spanish to conduct the interception operation, but when it was discovered that the weapons were headed for Yemen, the United States ordered the missiles to be released. There was speculation at the time that the United States did not want to risk damaging relations with a close partner in ongoing counterterror operations against al Qaeda and the Taliban. See Thomas E. Ricks and Peter Slevin, "Spain and U.S. Seize N. Korean Missiles," *Washington Post*, December 11, 2002; Michael Dobbs, "Waylaid at Sea: Launch of Policy; Handling of Scuds Raises Questions," *Washington Post*, December 13, 2002.

[29]Michael Evans, "Royal Marines Heading for Risky Task of Ferreting Out Bin Laden," *The Times* (London), October 26, 2001.

[30]Warren Hoge, "British Official Says Troops for Afghanistan Are Off High Alert," *New York Times*, November 27, 2001.

Anaconda.[31] The British government confirmed that these forces commenced operations between April 16 and 18, leading Operation Ptarmigan to search and clear a high valley in the Afghan mountains.[32] Royal Marines participated in three other major operations in southeastern Afghanistan—Operation Snipe, May 2–13, Operation Condor, May 17–22, and Operation Buzzard, May 29–July 9, 2002.[33]

Surprisingly, France and Romania were the only other European countries to contribute significant ground forces to the operation,[34] but these forces were limited in both size and scope. France's task force of 21st Marine Infantry Regiment soldiers conducted survey operations for repair of the Mazar-e-Sharif airport in November 2001, before deploying an infantry company to provide security there.[35] Romania contributed a detachment from a light infantry battalion in June 2002, including approximately 400 personnel, as well as a motorized infantry battalion.[36]

REVISITING NATO'S ROLE

The most notable feature of the European response to the events of September 11 is that it occurred primarily on a bilateral, and not a multilateral, basis. Despite the fact that NATO is one of the most institutionalized alliances ever created, with decades of experience in

---

[31]T. R. Reid, "Britain Set to Bulk Up Its Afghan Deployment," *Washington Post*, March 19, 2002.

[32]Operation Ptarmigan represented the first combat mission for the Royal Marines since the 1982 Falklands War. Peter Baker, "British Forces Lead New Afghan Mission," *Washington Post*, April 17, 2002.

[33]Operations Snipe and Buzzard both involved clearing mountains of Taliban and al Qaeda resistance, while Operation Condor involved providing support to Australian special forces operations. See "Operation Veritas," available at http://www. operations.mod.uk/veritas/forces.htm, and subsequent links to each specific operation.

[34]It should be noted here that Canada, a NATO member though not a European state, provided the largest coalition contingent of conventional ground forces. Canada contributed a Light Infantry Battle Group of more than 800 personnel, drawn from a battalion of Princess Patricia's Canadian Light Infantry. Department of Defense, "International Contributions to the War Against Terrorism"; U.S. Central Command, "International Contributions to the War on Terrorism."

[35]Department of Defense; U.S. Central Command.

[36]Department of Defense; U.S. Central Command.

fostering close ties among its members, the United States chose not to use NATO to organize its response to the attacks. NATO was unable to provide a command structure—or even substantial capabilities—that would override U.S. concerns about using the NATO machinery. European contributions were incorporated on a bilateral basis, but NATO as an organization remained limited to conducting patrols over the United States and deploying ships to the eastern Mediterranean.

This U.S. policy choice did not surprise many in the United States. Many U.S. policymakers believed that NATO's war in Kosovo was an unacceptable example of "war by committee," where political interference from the alliance's 19 members prevented a quick and decisive campaign. The policymakers were determined to retain sole command authority in Afghanistan, so that experience would not be repeated.[37] The deployment of the NATO AWACS demonstrates this point. The United States did not want to deploy the NATO AWACS directly to Afghanistan, because it did not want to involve the North Atlantic Council in any command decisions. Instead, the NATO AWACS backfilled U.S. assets so the assets could redeploy to Afghanistan.[38] A military official later described the U.S. decision in these terms: "If you were the US, would you want 18 other nations watering down your military planning?"[39]

However, many Europeans were dissatisfied with the small role that the alliance played in the response to the September 11 attacks and attributed it to U.S. unilateralism and arrogance. While they understood the need to ensure effective command and control, they felt

---

[37]Some analysts and participants in the Kosovo conflict, most notably General Wesley Clark, dispute the interpretation of Kosovo as a war by committee. See Clark, *Waging Modern War*, PublicAffairs, New York, 2001; Ivo H. Daalder and Michael E. O'Hanlon, *Winning Ugly: NATO's War to Save Kosovo*, Brookings Institution Press, Washington, D.C., 2000; Ivo H. Daalder and Philip R. Gordon, "Euro-Trashing," *Washington Post*, May 29, 2002.

[38]In fact, the decision to use NATO assets in this way generated NATO's own backfill requirement because the assets were already deployed in Bosnia. France agreed to use its national AWACS to backfill the NATO AWACS in Bosnia, so that the NATO AWACS could deploy to the United States and backfill the U.S. AWACS deploying to Afghanistan.

[39]Nicholas Fiorenza, "Alliance Solidarity," *Armed Forces Journal International*, December 2001, p. 22.

that they had given the United States unconditional political support through the invocation of Article 5 and that they should at least be consulted about the direction of the military campaign. In part, these frustrations resulted from the fact that the military campaign did not fit the model all had come to expect during the Cold War— that an invocation of Article 5 would lead the alliance members to join together and defeat a common enemy.[40] But these frustrations also reflected a fear that the U.S. decision to pursue the war on its own after invoking Article 5 would irrevocably weaken the core alliance principle of collective defense. A NATO ambassador from a large member state expressed his concerns as follows: "I don't blame the United States for handling the conflict in Afghanistan the way it did, given the complexity of that operation and the problems we saw when NATO managed the air war in Kosovo. I also understand that invoking Article 5 was a declaration of solidarity. But by declaring a situation of collective defense and failing to follow up, I fear that we may have undermined Article 5 forever; and therefore, I think that NATO has suffered as an alliance."[41]

TRANSATLANTIC TENSIONS OVER IRAQ

NATO, and transatlantic cooperation more broadly, suffered another blow when the United States shifted its attention from Afghanistan to Iraq. The diplomatic buildup to Operation Iraqi Freedom lasted more than a year, first involving divisions between the United States and the Europeans, and ultimately resulting in divisions within Europe itself. A detailed examination of the diplomatic events during that buildup is beyond our scope here, but there were two primary areas of disagreement: whether Iraq should be categorized as a problem of terrorism, and whether the United States had the right to take action in Iraq without explicit authorization from the United Nations (UN) Security Council.

---

[40]According to one senior NATO official, "Part of the problem was that no one had ever done this before, and all of us had an image from our schoolboy days that after Article 5 was invoked, the collective armies of the United States and Europe would march off together to slay a common foe. But this conflict is so unconventional that it didn't fit any of those stereotypes of what NATO was all about." Kitfield, "NATO Metamorphosis."

[41]Kitfield, "NATO Metamorphosis."

First, many European states disagreed with the U.S. argument that operations against Iraq should be the next step in the counterterror campaign. Despite the Bush administration's continuing insistence that Iraq supported international terrorism, including support of al Qaeda, most European states remained unconvinced that they faced a significant threat. Instead, they believed that Iraq posed a problem related to the proliferation of weapons of mass destruction. While this may seem like a semantic difference, these different conceptualizations of the problem led to extremely different policy preferences. The United States argued that Saddam Hussein's support for terrorism posed an imminent threat, and that regime change was the only way to mitigate this threat. Many of the European states, by contrast, believed that Saddam Hussein did not pose an imminent threat, but that he should not be allowed to achieve his long-term goal of procuring weapons of mass destruction. That objective required renewed UN weapons inspections but would not require regime change, at least in the short term.

The Europeans were encouraged by President Bush's speech to the United Nations on September 12, 2002,[42] in which he emphasized the importance of renewed WMD inspections, and by the unanimous passage of UN Security Council Resolution 1441, which provided a new mandate for the inspectors.[43] However, they grew increasingly disillusioned in early 2003, when the United States argued that it had the right to proceed with military action because Iraq was not fully cooperating with the weapons inspectors. Many Europeans argued that the inspections should be given more time, whereas the United States contended that Iraqi obstructions demonstrated that the inspections had once again failed.

The second major disagreement emerged during the debates on whether the UN would pass another resolution, in addition to Resolution 1441, that explicitly authorized the use of force against Iraq. France and Germany argued strongly and publicly that the inspections should continue, and when it became clear that the United

---

[42]The text of the speech is available at http://www.whitehouse.gov/news/releases/2002/09/20020912-1.html.

[43]For more on the diplomacy that led to Resolution 1441, see Karen DeYoung, "For Powell, a Long Path to a Victory," *Washington Post*, November 10, 2002.

States was no longer interested in supporting the inspections, they joined Russia in threatening to block any additional resolution.[44] The transatlantic war of words quickly escalated, with U.S. Secretary of Defense Donald Rumsfeld referring to France and Germany as "old Europe"[45] and chastising them for not being willing or able to tackle the most pressing security problems of the day.

As this rhetoric increased, several European countries grew increasingly uncomfortable with the idea that France and Germany were being seen as speaking for all of Europe. On January 30, 2003, the leaders of the Czech Republic, Denmark, Hungary, Italy, Poland, Portugal, Spain, and the United Kingdom published an op-ed piece in the *Wall Street Journal* supporting the U.S. position.[46] It stated that Iraq had demonstrated its unwillingness to cooperate with the UN inspectors and called on the international community to "safeguard world peace and security by ensuring that [the Iraqi] regime gives up its weapons of mass destruction."[47] Within the week, ten central and eastern European countries, all countries that had applied for NATO membership, issued their own statement supporting U.S. policies.[48] These statements demonstrated a funda-

---

[44]Julia Preston, "France Warns U.S. It Will Not Back Early War on Iraq," *New York Times*, January 21, 2003; Karen DeYoung and Colum Lynch, "Three Countries Vow to Block U.S. on Iraq," *Washington Post*, March 6, 2003; and Steven R. Weisman, "A Long, Winding Road to a Diplomatic Dead End," *New York Times*, March 17, 2003.

[45]"Secretary Rumsfeld Briefs at the Foreign Press Center," January 22, 2003, available at http://www.defenselink.mil/news/Jan2003/t01232003_t0122sdfpc.html.

[46]The *Wall Street Journal* reported that its editorial page contacted the Spanish, Italian, and British prime ministers in mid-January to see if they would be willing to explain their views and clarify the differences between their policies and those of France and Germany. Spanish Prime Minister Jose Maria Aznar contacted British Prime Minister Tony Blair, and the two agreed to cooperate on a statement. Aznar's office created an outline for the article, and the British completed the draft. The two leaders agreed that Aznar would ask the Portuguese and the Italians to participate in the article, while Blair would approach Denmark, the Netherlands, and the central European countries. The Netherlands declined to participate because its government was changing as the result of recent elections. Marc Champion, "Eight European Leaders Voice Their Support for U.S. on Iraq," *Wall Street Journal*, January 30, 2003.

[47]Jose Maria Aznar, Jose-Manuel Durao Barroso, Silvio Berlusconi, Tony Blair, Vaclav Havel, Peter Medgyessy, Leszek Miller, and Anders Fogh Rasmussen, "European Leaders in Support of U.S.," *Wall Street Journal*, January 30, 2003.

[48]The ten countries were Albania, Bulgaria, Croatia, Estonia, Latvia, Lithuania, Macedonia, Romania, Slovakia, and Slovenia. "New Allies Back U.S. Iraq Policy," *International Herald Tribune*, February 6, 2003.

mental split in European policy toward Iraq, from which it has not fully recovered. France and Germany continued opposing U.S. military action and chastising allies who disagreed until the day that Operation Iraqi Freedom commenced, whereas the United Kingdom made extensive military contributions to the coalition and smaller numbers of Danish and Polish forces also chose to participate.[49]

These disagreements also caused real political and military problems for NATO. In January 2003 the United States officially asked NATO to contribute to the campaign against Iraq, by backfilling U.S. troops redeploying from Europe to the Gulf, by helping to defend Turkey against possible retaliatory strikes from Iraq, and by assisting with postwar reconstruction and policing. Yet France, Germany, and Belgium opposed NATO undertaking any sort of operational planning, because they feared that taking such action before receiving a final report from the weapons inspectors would signal that they no longer believed in the possibility of a peaceful solution and would commit them to the operation by default. They were particularly concerned about the proposal for NATO to help defend Turkey by providing it with AWACS radar planes, Patriot antimissile batteries, and antibiological and antichemical warfare units.[50]

On February 6, NATO Secretary General Robertson tried to break the stalemate over Turkish assistance by invoking the silence procedure, which meant that such assistance to Turkey would be automatically approved unless one or more allies explicitly objected.[51] The silence procedure had often helped the allies overcome differences in the past,[52] but on February 10, France, Germany, and Belgium expressed

---

[49]Poland contributed special forces, while Denmark contributed a submarine to monitor Iraqi intelligence and to provide early warning. The Czech Republic and Slovakia also contributed antibiological and antichemical warfare units, but the units remained based in Kuwait and did not participate in direct military operations against Iraq. Condoleezza Rice, "Our Coalition," *Wall Street Journal*, March 26, 2003.

[50]Philip Shishkin, "European NATO Leaders Say War Planning Undermines U.N.," *Wall Street Journal*, January 21, 2003; Champion,"Eight European Leaders Voice Their Support for U.S. on Iraq."

[51]Keith B. Richburg, "Key Allies Not Won Over By Powell," *Washington Post*, February 7, 2003.

[52]The silence procedure had often helped the allies overcome some of their differences in the past, including during the 1999 war over Kosovo. See John E. Peters,

formal opposition to the proposal to provide assistance to Turkey. That same day, Turkey invoked Article 4 of the NATO Charter, which requires the allies to consult if one of them perceives a threat to its security. This marked the first time that the Article 4 consultation mechanism had ever been invoked, and Turkey clearly hoped that the seriousness of that action would help to force action. Yet France, Germany, and Belgium turned down this direct request, reiterating their position that such action was premature and would seem to commit NATO to war before the inspectors finished their work.[53] In response, the United States announced that it would join willing allies in deploying defensive equipment to Turkey, even if that action was not taken within the NATO framework.[54]

Once it became clear that the North Atlantic Council would not be able to reach agreement on assistance to Turkey, Secretary General Robertson shrewdly chose to raise the question within NATO's Defense Planning Committee (DPC)—a body that does not include France because France is not part of the alliance's integrated military structure. On February 16, after several lengthy negotiating sessions, Germany and Belgium acquiesced and agreed to provide the defensive assistance to Turkey described above.[55] Robertson later revealed that he had written a letter to the heads of state of the alliance, warning them that the credibility of the alliance was at stake on this issue. After the DPC approved the action, Robertson argued that "the alliance has been damaged but it is not broken," for it had ultimately reached a decision.[56] Despite this relatively upbeat assessment, the debate over assistance to Turkey revealed a fundamental disagreement within the alliance, which could not be overcome even once Turkey invoked the provisions of Article 4. The facts remain that the North Atlantic Council was not able to reach a decision on this criti-

---

Stuart Johnson, Nora Bensahel, Timothy Liston, and Traci Williams, *European Contributions to Operation Allied Force*, RAND, MR-1391-AF, 2001, pp. 48–49.

[53]Peter Finn, "U.S.-Europe Rifts Widen Over Iraq," *Washington Post*, February 11, 2003; Craig S. Smith with Richard Bernstein, "3 NATO Members and Russia Resist U.S. on Iraq Plans," *New York Times*, February 11, 2003.

[54]Finn, "U.S.-Europe Rifts Widen Over Iraq."

[55]Philip Shishkin, "Robertson, NATO's Head, Seeks to Fix Credibility," *Wall Street Journal*, February 19, 2003.

[56]Michael R. Gordon, "NATO Chief Says Alliance Needs Role in Afghanistan," *New York Times*, February 21, 2003.

cal issue and that the issue could be settled only in a forum that did not include one of Europe's largest countries, posing real questions about the future role of the alliance.

What do the debates over Iraq indicate about the future of counterterror cooperation with Europe? First, it indicates the tremendous difficulty in reaching consensus agreement on the next steps in the counterterror campaign. It was easy to reach an international consensus on the need to go after al Qaeda, particularly after the September 11 attacks, because most states perceived al Qaeda as a fundamental threat to their sovereignty. Yet few other potential targets of the counterterror campaign will inspire such a unified international response. Iraq demonstrated the difficulties of trying to reach international consensus on which groups and states are the legitimate targets of counterterror operations.

Second, the divisions that emerged within NATO have raised significant questions about the future role of the alliance. The unwillingness of several members to support Turkey's request for assistance, even after officially invoking Article 4 of the North Atlantic Treaty, has undermined the alliance's credibility to its members, invitees, and even nonmembers. As NATO seeks to mend the damage, it becomes increasingly unlikely that the alliance will adopt countering terrorism as one of its new missions, as discussed in the following chapter.

Chapter Three

THE EVOLVING ROLE OF EUROPEAN INSTITUTIONS

The long-term success of the counterterror campaign will depend on concerted cooperation from the European states. Their strong economies and democratic protections make them attractive locations for terrorist planning—as already demonstrated on September 11. Individual states will continue to make important contributions in identifying and tracking down suspected terrorists, but the ever-increasing interdependence among the European states will also require concerted multilateral action to prevent terrorists from hiding their activities in the gaps between sovereign authorities.

Interestingly, the European Union may be a more helpful partner in certain aspects of the long-term campaign against terrorism than NATO. Although terrorism is a major security challenge facing states on both sides of the Atlantic, NATO remains torn by disagreements on the extent to which counterterrorism should shape its agenda. The European Union, by contrast, is strengthening cooperation in law enforcement and other areas in ways that may prove to be crucial in preventing future terrorist actions.

RETHINKING NATO'S AGENDA

The September 11 attacks forced NATO not only to think about its immediate response, but also to consider the long-term challenges posed by terrorism and the alliance's capability to respond to terrorist threats. During the late 1990s, and particularly during the preparations for the Washington Summit in April 1999, the United States encouraged NATO to include counterterrorism as one of its core tasks. Yet France and several other European allies opposed this idea, because they feared that it would transform NATO into a European police force instead of a military alliance. Retired German General Klaus Naumann, the former head of NATO's Military Committee, recalled one meeting where Spain, Turkey, and the United Kingdom—all countries that face domestic terrorist threats—defeated a proposal for NATO to play a role in countering terrorism.[1] After September 11, the United States and France quickly agreed that there was no reason to change the 1999 Strategic Concept, the most recent statement of NATO's purpose and strategy, because that would involve the allies in lengthy debates about the exact language and scope of NATO's role. Instead, they agreed that the Strategic Concept could now be reinterpreted to include countering terror as a core task, affecting the vital security interests of all members.[2] The other allies quickly agreed.

Despite this initial agreement, the NATO allies spent several months debating the proper way to describe NATO's role in countering terrorism. For example, in the preparations for the foreign ministers meeting in December 2001, France opposed the U.S. proposal to express counterterrorism as a "fundamental security task" of the alliance.[3] They reached a semantic compromise by splitting up the phrase, with the final communiqué from the meeting stating that meeting the terrorist challenge is "fundamental to our security."[4] An even more significant debate erupted over the language used in the final communiqué for the Reykjavik ministerial meeting held in May 2002. Several alliance members wanted to include a statement that NATO was prepared to combat terrorism globally and that there would be no limits on NATO's global reach for such operations. France repeated its long-standing objections to giving NATO an explicitly global role, and argued that Article 5 already authorized the alliance to address threats that originate outside the alliance's bor-

---

[1]Matthew Kaminski, "NATO's Low Priority on Terrorism Leaves It Ill Prepared for Latest War," *Wall Street Journal*, October 5, 2001.

[2]Interviews with NATO officials, July 2002.

[3]Interviews with NATO officials, July 2002.

[4]For the full text of the foreign ministers' communiqué, see "NATO's Response to Terrorism: Statement issued at the ministerial meeting of the North Atlantic Council held at NATO Headquarters, Brussels, on 6 December 2001," Press Release M-NAC-2(2001)159, December 6, 2001.

ders.[5] The final communiqué included a compromise proposed by the French, which included an implicit, but not explicit, statement of a global role: "NATO must be able to field forces that can move quickly to wherever they are needed, sustain operations over distance and time, and achieve their objectives."[6] These distinctions may seem somewhat inconsequential, but they do reveal significant differences about the ways that the member states view the future role of the alliance in combating terrorism.

NATO has taken some short-term steps to address the problem of terrorism, such as establishing an internal terrorism task force to coordinate the work of the many different offices within the NATO staff.[7] It is also pursuing several initiatives that are designed to improve its long-term counterterror capabilities, including adopting a military concept for combating terrorism, launching the new capabilities initiative, considering a NATO Rapid Response Force, addressing WMD threats, improving civil-military emergency planning and consequence management, and enhancing cooperative relationships and training with partners.

The Military Concept for Combating Terrorism

In December 2001, the NATO defense ministers tasked NATO's two military authorities—the Supreme Allied Commander Europe (SACEUR) and the Supreme Allied Commander Atlantic (SACLANT)—to produce a concept for defending against terrorism.[8] After receiving political guidance, military guidance, and a threat as-

---

[5]Interviews with NATO officials, July 2002.

[6]"Final Communiqué: Ministerial Meeting of the North Atlantic Council Held in Reykjavik on 14 May 2002," Press Release M-NAC-1(2002)59, May 14, 2002.

[7]The task force, led by the Assistant Secretary General for Defense Planning and Operations, coordinates the work of the International Military Staff, the Division of Political Affairs, the Division of Defense Support, the Director of Civil-Military Planning, and the Office of Information and Press, among others. It focuses on short-term measures that can help counter the terrorist threat, such as improving cyberdefense. It also produces a biweekly status report for the allies on NATO's counterterrorism initiatives, so that they are all aware of alliance activities in this area. Interview with NATO official, July 2002.

[8]All information on the Military Concept for Combating Terrorism comes from interviews with NATO officials, July 2002, and with U.S officials, December 2002.

sessment from the NATO staff, the two military commands jointly produced a draft Military Concept for Combating Terrorism, which was officially approved during the November 2002 Prague Summit. The concept includes four pillars—antiterrorism, consequence management, counterterrorism, and military cooperation with civil authorities—and suggests the appropriate NATO role for each one.

Antiterrorism. The concept defines antiterrorism as defensive measures that decrease vulnerability. It leaves primary responsibility for these measures to the member states. NATO can supplement national efforts by establishing a standard threat-warning system, and it may adopt measures to improve air and maritime protection.

Consequence management. Once an attack has taken place, member states will retain responsibility for responding to the attack and mitigating its effects. NATO's military forces might be able to support civilian efforts perhaps by establishing alliance requirements for national capabilities or by establishing standing forces dedicated to consequence management that could be used when requested by national authorities.

Counterterrorism. The concept envisages two types of offensive alliance actions to decrease vulnerabilities to terrorism—one where NATO is in the lead, and one where NATO supports national authorities. For the former, NATO needs to improve its military capabilities, as discussed below. It also needs to consider standing joint and combined forces for counterterror operations and expanding the capabilities of the standing naval force. When NATO is supporting national authorities (whether they are operating alone or as part of a coalition of the willing), NATO can backfill national requirements, as it did for Operation Noble Eagle, and it can enable operations by providing host-nation support, access to bases, and blanket overflight rights. Its ongoing efforts to engage partner nations can also facilitate those nations' roles in any potential counterterror operations.

Military cooperation with civil authorities. Even though many alliance members remain wary about giving NATO a role in this area, the concept stresses that NATO must be prepared to interact with national civil authorities and international organizations. Any major terrorist attack, and particularly one that involved biological, chemical, or nuclear weapons, could overwhelm the response capabilities of any individual state, and NATO must be prepared to lend assistance in such cases.

From these four pillars, NATO military authorities then derived a number of essential military capabilities for the alliance, including improving deployability, precision engagement, and surveillance and force protection; and establishing effective intelligence as well as civil-military interaction.

Although this concept establishes important principles about NATO's role in combating terrorism, the overall role of the alliance remains fairly limited. National authorities retain primary responsibility in most areas, and the concept does not envisage any revolutionary changes to the alliance's structure or capabilities. Now that the concept has been approved, NATO's military authorities can start developing specific concepts of operations and operational plans, which may provide more defined roles for the alliance. However, based on the guidance they have been given, it seems as though NATO's role in combating terrorism will consist mostly of supporting the individual efforts of its member states rather than defining a new role for the alliance in this area.

The Prague Capabilities Commitment

The growing capabilities gap between the United States and its European allies has garnered a lot of attention in recent months, in the press, in policy circles, and within the alliance itself.[9] NATO launched the Defense Capabilities Initiative (DCI) at the April 1999 Washington Summit in an effort to narrow this gap, but the DCI is widely regarded as having been too broad and unfocused. The unexpectedly quick U.S. military victory over the Taliban in the fall of 2001 and the inability of most allies to contribute significant capabilities renewed interest in this important question. The capabilities gap became one of the main issues discussed at the February 2002 Munich Conference on Security Policy, particularly after Secretary

---

[9]See, for example, David S. Yost, "The NATO Capabilities Gap and the European Union," *Survival*, Vol. 42, No. 4, Winter 2000–2001, pp. 97–128; and Klaus Naumann, "How to Close the Capabilities Gap," *Wall Street Journal*, May 23, 2002.

General Robertson warned that Europe risked settling for the status of a "military pygmy" if its military capabilities did not improve.[10]

At the November 2002 Prague Summit, NATO officially adopted a new capabilities initiative. The process for developing this initiative began before the September 11 attacks, but it was reworked after the attacks to emphasize capabilities useful for combating terrorism as well as more traditional defense tasks.[11] This initiative, known as the Prague Capabilities Commitment (PCC), emphasizes improving capabilities in eight specific areas:

- Defense against chemical, biological, nuclear, and radiological weapons

- Intelligence, surveillance, and target acquisition

- Air-to-ground surveillance

- Command, control, and communications

- Combat effectiveness, including precision-guided munitions and suppression of enemy air defense

- Strategic air and sea lift

- Air-to-air refueling

- Deployable combat support and combat service support units.[12]

The PCC, unlike the DCI, gives individual members the opportunity to tailor their contributions by focusing on specific capabilities. Germany, for example, is taking the lead in building a strategic lift consortium, analyzing the benefits of leasing transport aircraft in the short term and pooling the consortium's airlift resources in the long term. The Netherlands is leading an effort that includes Canada, Denmark, Belgium, and Norway to pool purchases of precision

---

[10]Joseph Fitchett, "Pentagon in a League of Its Own," *International Herald Tribune*, February 4, 2002; Philip Shishkin, "Europe Must Strengthen Military, Say Concerned Defense Officials," *Wall Street Journal*, February 4, 2002; Vago Muradian, "NATO Remains Key, But U.S. Ready to Fight Antiterror War Without Europe," *Defense Daily International*, February 8, 2002.

[11]Interviews with NATO officials, July 2002.

[12]Prague Summit Declaration, NATO Press Release (2002)127, November 21, 2002.

munitions. Spain is leading a consortium that will attempt to garner support for leasing up to 100 aerial tankers. Canada, France, Italy, the Netherlands, Spain, and Turkey have all made individual commitments to buy unmanned aerial vehicles.[13] However, U.S. officials were somewhat disappointed with the outcome of this initiative, because they had hoped that the other NATO allies would make commitments and pledge to increase their defense spending.[14]

It is too soon to tell whether these efforts will succeed. Although they are certainly a step in the right direction, little progress has been made to date. Nevertheless, these efforts are designed to address some of the most pressing immediate shortfalls as well as improving capabilities for the long term.

The NATO Response Force

Two months before the Prague Summit, Secretary of Defense Donald Rumsfeld proposed that NATO create a new rapid response force. During the September 2002 meeting of NATO defense ministers in Berlin, Rumsfeld argued that NATO needed to develop the capability to respond quickly and effectively to terrorism and other emerging threats outside Europe's borders. He warned his colleagues, "If NATO does not have a force that's quick and agile, that can deploy in days or weeks rather than months or years, then it will not have capabilities to offer the world in the 21st century."[15] Alhough France expressed some concerns, the defense ministers generally expressed their support for the proposal.[16]

During the Prague Summit, NATO formally decided to establish the NATO Response Force (NRF), which would be "a technologically advanced, flexible, deployable, interoperable and sustainable force including land, sea, and air elements ready to move quickly to wher-

---

[13]Nicholas Fiorenza, "NATO to Adopt Capabilities Plan," *Defense News*, November 18–24, 2002; Fact Sheet, "NATO: Building New Capabilities for New Challenges," The White House, Office of the Press Secretary, November 21, 2002.

[14]Interview with U.S. government official, December 2002.

[15]Steven Erlanger, "Rumsfeld Urges NATO to Set Up Strike Force," *New York Times*, September 25, 2002.

[16]Bradley Graham and Robert G. Kaiser, "NATO Ministers Back U.S. Plan for Rapid Reaction Force," *Washington Post*, September 25, 2002.

ever needed."[17] It would be capable of conducting the full range of military missions, sustaining itself for 30 days, and rotating in assignment for six months. The exact composition of the force would be determined by mission needs, but it could notionally include enough air assets to conduct 200 combat sorties per day, a brigade-sized ground force, and maritime forces up to the size of a NATO standing naval force—approximately 21,000 personnel in all.[18] The Prague Summit Declaration calls for the NRF to achieve initial operating capacity by October 2004 and full operational capacity by October 2006.[19]

While the allies support the NRF in principle, it remains unclear whether they will develop the capabilities necessary to make it work. The Europeans do not currently possess those capabilities, and even if the PCC is successful, these capabilities will not be fielded until the end of the decade at the earliest. Some observers note that the Europeans have still not fulfilled their commitments to build the capabilities necessary for an EU rapid response force, which has the more limited mandate of conducting peacekeeping and peace enforcement missions instead of high-intensity combat.[20] The NRF, if successful, could prove a useful tool in countering terrorist threats around the world, but it remains to be seen whether the allies are willing to devote the resources necessary to make it a reality.

Addressing WMD Threats

The Prague Summit also included discussions about ways to improve the alliance's ability to deal with terrorist threats, particularly those that involve weapons of mass destruction. The North Atlantic Council endorsed the implementation of five different initiatives to improve NATO's capabilities to defend against nuclear, biological, and chemical (NBC) attacks, which included

- Developing a prototype deployable NBC analytic lab

---

[17]Prague Summit Declaration.

[18]Fact Sheet, "NATO: Building New Capabilities for New Challenges."

[19]Prague Summit Declaration.

[20]Interviews with U.S. government officials, December 2002.

- Developing a prototype NBC event response team
- Creating a virtual Center of Excellence for NBC weapons defense
- Establishing a NATO biological and chemical defense stockpile
- Developing a disease surveillance system.[21]

These initiatives are an important step forward, in an area that goes beyond NATO's traditional areas of responsibility. Yet even if they are successfully implemented, NATO's ability to detect and respond to an attack involving WMD will still remain limited. NATO's Weapons of Mass Destruction Center has a staff of only 12 people, who already have many other responsibilities. It is unlikely that the office will be able to serve as much more than a clearinghouse for information sharing among the allies. More important, all of the initiatives described above will focus solely on deployed military forces, *not* on protecting civilian populations.[22] Some member states believe that primary responsibility in this area should remain with the national governments and not be entrusted to the alliance. While there are compelling reasons for this preference, it does limit these states' ability to improve their prevention and detection activities through intelligence sharing and other cooperative measures.

Civil-Military Emergency Planning and Consequence Management

Whereas the WMD Center focuses on preventing and detecting WMD use, the Civil-Military Planning Directorate includes responsibility for consequence management. However, alliance capabilities in this area remain limited. NATO does hold an annual consequence management exercise, called CMX, but it generates few concrete lessons at the operational level. Few people within the directorate focus exclusively on this issue area, and those who do are volunteers or are seconded and paid for by other organizations within the alliance structure. This topic is also on the Prague agenda, but it remains far less developed than the other issues discussed here.[23]

---

[21]Prague Summit Declaration.

[22]Interviews with NATO officials, July 2002.

[23]Interviews with NATO officials, July 2002.

Why is there such resistance within NATO regarding consequence management? Part of the reason stems from a desire to address this issue at the national rather than the alliance level, as described above. Yet there is another aspect here, concerning the distribution of responsibilities among European institutions. Although many NATO members would like to see the alliance take more responsibility in this area, France has opposed efforts to give that responsibility to the alliance. France wants NATO to remain a military organization and prefers to build civilian capabilities for consequence management within the European Union. France has consistently argued that NATO must not develop its own consequence management capabilities until the EU has developed capabilities in this area, and then the two organizations can jointly determine how to proceed. Yet the EU has been quite slow in determining organizational responsibility for consequence management, as a result of turf battles within the European Council, within the European Commission, and between the Council and Commission. Critics charge that France is deliberately preventing NATO from developing competence in this area in order to ensure that the EU can step in to fill the gap. They argue that NATO cooperates with many international organizations on civil-military emergency planning—including the United Nations, the Organization for Security and Cooperation in Europe, and the World Health Organization among others—but that NATO-EU cooperation on consequence management remains extremely limited.[24]

Whatever the reasons behind the French policy, it has prevented NATO from improving its consequence management capabilities. Until the EU develops its own capabilities, or the French policy changes, national governments will maintain primary responsibility for consequence management. Some NATO officials fear that national capabilities for consequence management will prove woefully inadequate after a WMD attack, particularly for the smaller alliance members, and that the members will naturally turn to NATO for assistance. Yet consequence management is not an official military

---

[24]To date, NATO and the EU have held two joint meetings on civil-military emergency planning, in November 2001 and May 2002. Yet few concrete initiatives resulted from the meetings, and NATO officials say that the EU often rejects their overtures to build a dialogue and expert contacts between the two institutions. Interviews with NATO officials, July 2002.

task for the alliance, so NATO has no prepared response for such a contingency. These officials worry that the alliance will lose its legitimacy among the European people if it cannot provide assistance quickly and effectively in the aftermath of a WMD attack.

Cooperative Relationships with Partners

One of NATO's great strengths is that it promotes cooperation not only among its members but with partner states as well. NATO's outreach programs provide a good opportunity to strengthen cooperation against terrorism among the partner states, particularly because the institutional mechanisms for cooperation already exist.[25] The Partnership for Peace (PfP) is the oldest of these mechanisms, established in 1994 to foster cooperation with the states of eastern Europe and the former Soviet Union. However, the character and purpose of the PfP may change significantly in the coming years. Seven current PfP members were invited to join the alliance during the Prague Summit, and the remaining PfP members are not likely to join NATO in either the near or medium term.[26] Thus, the PfP will have to reorient its activities so that they focus less on preparing for NATO membership. One possible direction for future cooperation is to address common threats such as terrorism. NATO also maintains special partnerships with Russia and Ukraine, which could also be used to address issues related to terrorism.

The Mediterranean Dialogue may become the most important of these regional partnerships for the long-term struggle against terrorism—its seven non-NATO members are Algeria, Egypt, Israel, Jordan, Mauritania, Morocco, and Tunisia. Terrorism has not traditionally been an area of cooperation within the Mediterranean Dialogue, and its 2002 Work Program states only that "NATO is considering possibilities for consultation on terrorism with interested Mediterranean

---

[25]Interview with NATO official, July 2002.

[26]The seven countries that have been invited to join NATO are Bulgaria, Estonia, Latvia, Lithuania, Romania, Slovakia, and Slovenia. The remaining PfP members include Albania, Armenia, Austria, Azerbaijan, Belarus, Croatia, Finland, Georgia, Ireland, Kazakhstan, Kyrgyzstan, Moldova, the former Yugoslav Republic of Macedonia, Russia, Sweden, Switzerland, Tajikistan, Turkmenistan, Ukraine, and Uzbekistan.

Dialogue countries."[27] Nevertheless, over the long term, the Mediterranean Dialogue could develop programs of cooperation in this important area that supplement what the United States and the other NATO members are able to achieve on a bilateral basis.

STRENGTHENING THE EUROPEAN UNION

An unexpected outcome of the September 11 attacks was that it spurred further integration within the European Union, particularly within the law enforcement and financial areas. The EU had been developing its competency in these areas since 1999, but many proposals had stagnated in the face of disagreements among the member states. The September 11 attacks catapulted these issues to the top of the European agenda, because increased financial and law enforcement cooperation are a crucial part of preventing terrorist attacks from occurring.

On September 21, 2001, the EU heads of state issued an action plan against terrorism that contains a broad blueprint of EU counterterrorism activities. It calls for the EU to focus on five issues—enhancing police cooperation, developing international legal instruments, ending terrorist funding, strengthening air security, and coordinating the EU's global action—and identifies specific measures that should be undertaken in each issue area. It also calls for enhanced cooperation inside the EU, as well as between the EU and other countries.[28] More than 60 of the specific recommendations are tracked in a document that the EU refers to as the Road Map, which is revised every month to include progress in that particular area and to identify next steps toward fulfilling the recommendation.[29]

The EU has not made a significant contribution in the military and intelligence elements of the counterterrorism campaign, because it has few institutional capabilities to do so. Although its members

---

[27]Mediterranean Dialogue Work Programme, available at http://www.nato.int/meddial/2002/mdwp-2002.pdf.

[28]"Conclusions and Plan of Action of the Extraordinary European Council Meeting on 21 September 2001," Press Release SN 140/01, September 21, 2001.

[29]Interview with EU official, July 2002.

certainly possess these capabilities individually, the EU as an institution does not. The Common Foreign and Security Policy (CFSP), still in an early stage of development, currently coordinates the policies of individual members instead of establishing a truly common policy. Efforts to build a military force of 60,000 soldiers as part of the European Security and Defense Policy (ESDP) are progressing slowly, having stalled for more than two years because of disagreements about the extent of its links to NATO.[30] These issues were largely resolved between December 2002 and March 2003;[31] at the end of March, the EU took command of NATO's peacekeeping mission in Macedonia.[32] Although these are notable steps forward, the EU's military force will likely not participate in high-intensity counterterror operations because it was designed for peacekeeping and peace enforcement missions.

However, the EU may be able to contribute to judicial and law enforcement cooperation, particularly through the Directorate of Justice and Home Affairs (JHA). JHA, which is also known as the "third pillar" of the EU, operates according to intergovernmental principles of decisionmaking, which means that any common policies must emerge through a consensus of the member states and cannot be dictated by EU institutions in Brussels.[33] Developing common JHA policies has therefore been a slow and tedious process, requiring lengthy consultations and compromises among the 15 members and often resulting in vague declarations. However, that process has been revitalized since September 11, with the EU members realizing that common police and judicial efforts are absolutely

---

[30]For more on the history and potential for an EU military force, see Robert E. Hunter, *The European Security and Defense Policy: NATO's Companion—or Competitor?* RAND, MR-1463-NDRI/RE, 2002.

[31]Turkey had blocked such an agreement because it did not want the EU to be able to assist Greece with military operations involving Cyprus. Turkey withdrew its objections when Greece and Cyprus agreed that the EU would not be involved in military planning for issues involving the island. Joseph Fitchett, "NATO Agrees to Help New EU Force," *International Herald Tribune,* December 16, 2002; Anthee Carassava, "European Union and NATO Sign Pact," *New York Times,* March 15, 2003.

[32]Misha Savic, "EU Peacekeepers Arrive in Macedonia," *Washington Post,* April 1, 2003.

[33]For more on the development of the third pillar, see John D. Occhipinti, *The Politics of EU Police Cooperation,* Lynne Rienner Publishers, Boulder, CO, 2003, especially Chapter 3.

crucial to identifying and locating terrorists operating within their borders. As two observers of European politics noted, "The impact of 11 September was that existing arrangements were reinvigorated, and that draft agreements sailed through a political window of opportunity."[34] The most important initiatives in this area include adopting the Framework Decision on Combating Terrorism, adopting a common arrest warrant, increasing the role of Europol, strengthening Eurojust, and combating terrorist financing.

The Framework Decision on Combating Terrorism

On September 19, 2001, the European Commission proposed a Framework Decision on Combating Terrorism, which entered into force in June 2002.[35] Before that time, only six of the 15 EU members had legislation on their books that criminalized terrorism.[36] The Framework Decision adopts a uniform definition of terrorism, based on the one used by the United Nations, and imposes uniform criminal penalties for terrorism throughout the European Union. In conjunction with this framework, the EU has adopted a list of groups and individuals who are suspected of being involved in terrorist activities.[37] The Framework Decision enables the EU to take proactive measures, such as freezing assets, against the groups and individuals on that list, instead of waiting for a specific crime to be committed.[38]

The Framework Decision does not grant the EU any new supranational powers to combat terrorism. Instead, it enhances efforts to

---

[34]Monica Den Boer and Jörg Monar, "Keynote Article: 11 September and the Challenge of Global Terrorism to the EU as a Security Actor," *Journal of Common Market Studies*, Vol. 40, Annual Review, 2002, p. 21.

[35]"Proposal for a Council Framework Decision on Combating Terrorism," COM(2001) 521 final, Brussels, September 19, 2001; "Council Framework Decision of June 13 2002 on Combating Terrorism," 2002/475/JHA.

[36]Kristin Archick, *Europe and Counterterrorism: Strengthening Police and Judicial Cooperation*, Congressional Research Service Report to Congress, July 23, 2002, p. CRS-2; Occhipinti, p. 149.

[37]This list was first adopted on December 27, 2001, and has been modified since then. See, for example, "Decision Adopted by Written Procedure: Fight Against Terrorism—Updated List," 8549/02 (Presse 121), Brussels, May 3, 2002.

[38]Dorine Dubois, "The Attacks of 11 September: EU-US Cooperation Against Terrorism in the Field of Justice and Home Affairs," *European Foreign Policy Review*, Vol. 7, 2002, p. 323; interviews with U.S. and EU officials, July 2002.

combat terrorism by setting standards that its member states are expected to follow. In one sense, the EU role in defining and criminalizing terrorism is similar to its role in customs policy: EU institutions determine common policies but leave the enforcement of those policies to national judges and police authorities.[39] Yet by establishing common standards, the EU is making it harder for terrorists to conduct their activities in the most legally permissive areas of the European Union. The groups and individuals named on the official EU terrorist list will now face identical criminal charges throughout the European Union, and the Framework Decision enables member states to disrupt the terrorist activities before any crime has been committed.

The Common Arrest Warrant

The European Union began discussing adoption of a common arrest warrant long before the September 11 attacks, in an effort to address terrorism as well as a number of other transnational crimes. Yet the idea had stagnated in the face of opposition from several member states. As one observer put it, the common warrant had become "another in-basket item for water cooler discussion" but not real action.[40] September 11 revitalized interest in this measure, particularly once the extent of the hijackers' activities in Europe became known. On September 19, the European Commission once again proposed the idea of a common arrest warrant, and there was a high-level political commitment within the EU to move forward quickly.[41] EU officials reached agreement on the warrant on December 12, 2001, and agreed that it would come into force no later than January 2004.[42]

---

[39]If member states do not comply with EU policies, they can be sued either in their own national courts or in the European Court of Justice. Interviews with EU officials, July 2002.

[40]Interview with U.S. government official, July 2002.

[41]Donald J. McNeil, Jr., "Europe Moves to Toughen Laws to Fight Terrorism," *New York Times*, September 20, 2001.

[42]"Laeken European Council: Extradition will no longer be necessary between EU member states," December 14–15, 2001, available at http://europa.eu.int/comm/justice_home/news/laeken_council/en/mandat_en.htm. Six EU members—Belgium, France, Luxembourg, Portugal, Spain, and the United Kingdom—also announced that

Because it will effectively put an end to the often protracted extradition fights among the members of the European Union for the 32 offenses covered by the warrant, the common arrest warrant is a major step toward the creation of a single judicial area. The judiciary of each state will be able to issue arrest warrants that are recognized by all other members, and it will be able to transfer arrested suspects directly to the state that issued the warrant.[43] These provisions will require major changes in domestic legal codes, and in many cases they will require constitutional amendments. Only four out of the current 15 members allow for extradition of their citizens, and four member states ban such extradition outright. Germany has "reinterpreted" its constitution to allow for such extradition, but Denmark, Italy, and Austria will likely require constitutional amendments for the arrest warrant to enter into force.[44]

Even though the common arrest warrant is not scheduled to enter into force until 2004, and full implementation may take even longer, it has the potential to become an important tool in the long-term struggle against terrorism. When fully implemented, it will enable judicial authorities to transfer suspects among EU members just as they currently transfer suspects between districts within their own countries, eliminating the lengthy and cumbersome formal extradition process. It will become increasingly difficult for terrorists—as well as others involved in transnational crime—to take advantage of differing legal standards in Europe by basing their activities in less-restrictive states.

Increasing the Role of Europol

The European Police Office, otherwise known as Europol, was established during the 1990s as a center for collecting, analyzing, and dis-

---

they would seek to introduce the common arrest warrant ahead of the deadline in 2003. Occhipinti, p. 172.

[43] "Laeken European Council . . . . "

[44]The German constitution prohibits extradition to foreign countries, but the government has argued that other EU members are not really considered "foreign" anymore, and therefore the common arrest warrant is permitted by the constitution. Interviews with U.S. officials, June and July 2002.

seminating information.[45] For most of its history, it has been more of a coordination office than an operational headquarters, providing assistance to its members instead of acting independently. Europol cannot conduct its own investigations, undertake searches, or arrest suspects. It operates through a network of liaison officers who are seconded from their national institutions and therefore remain accountable under their respective national laws. Member states can withhold information from Europol when they believe that their national security interests outweigh the benefits of international cooperation.[46] Immediately after September 11, Europol's director, Jürgen Storbeck, stated that Europol could do more to counter terrorism if member states would be more willing to share information with his organization.[47]

Europol's mandate was expanded somewhat after the September 11 attacks. On September 12, 2001, Europol established a crisis center to coordinate and share information about the terrorist attacks, and it soon created a terrorism task force to provide broad analysis and threat assessments. During the following months, it gained the authority to ask police forces of member states to launch investigations and to share information with Interpol, the United States, and others.[48] It also gained additional financial resources to help cover the cost of the counterterror mission, with its budget increasing from €33.2 million in 2001 to €51.7 million in 2002.[49] However, it remains to be seen whether these measures will substantially increase Europol's authority over its members. Europol may now ask its members to launch investigations, but it cannot order them to do

---

[45]Europol operated informally for a number of years before it became fully operational in July 1999. For more information on Europol's history, see Occhipinti, especially Chapters 3 and 4.

[46]Occhipinti, pp. 2 and 61.

[47]In an interview, Storbeck called on the EU member states to "simply provide us with what we need for our work: information." He also called for increased funding, noting that "if Europol is to do more than simply analyze data, then it must be better equipped." Occhipinti, p. 149.

[48]Occhipinti, pp. 149, 165–166, and 198; interviews with EU officials, July 2002.

[49]The amount of money allocated for operational expenses increased from €23.7 million in 2001 to €34.6 million in 2002. Occhipinti, p. 199.

so.[50] Europol personnel may not detain or arrest suspects, and may participate in investigations of crimes only within their specified mandate.[51] The terrorism task force has been criticized for short-comings in handling real-time data, leading to speculation that the task force may be restructured or perhaps even absorbed into Europol's larger functions.[52]

Europol's current capabilities remain limited to a coordination role, largely because its members disagree about its proper purpose and scope. Some members, including Germany, would like to see it evolve into an organization like the FBI over time, with an independent investigative role. Other members, including the United Kingdom, oppose such an evolution, preferring individual members to retain investigative authority and having Europol simply coordinate their efforts. Furthermore, the police forces of the EU members generally view Europol with a great deal of suspicion, believing that it infringes on their authority and autonomy.[53] These issues limit Europol's counterterrorism role, since Europol cannot initiate international investigations and must rely instead on the individual efforts of its members. Furthermore, some members have been reluctant to share information about terrorism with Europol, preferring to work through state-to-state contacts. Europol thus often lacks a complete understanding of current threat levels, international connections among suspected terrorists, and the counterterrorism efforts of its own members.[54]

Despite these problems, Europol may still emerge as an important part of European counterterrorism efforts in the next decade. Even if Europol does not gain supranational authority to launch investigations on its own, it could strengthen its capabilities to coordinate the

---

[50]Member states that refuse to comply with such requests must respond in writing and explain why they are refusing to do so, which does impose some costs for noncompliance. Interviews with U.S. government officials, June and July 2002.

[51]Archick, p. CRS-3.

[52]Interviews with U.S. and EU officials, July 2002.

[53]As Jürgen Storbeck, the director of Europol, explained: "For a policeman, information about his own case is like property. He is even reluctant to give it to his chief or to another department, let alone giving it to the regional or national services. For an international body like Europol, it is very difficult." Quoted in Archick, p. CRS-9.

[54]Interviews with U.S. and EU officials, July 2002.

individual efforts of its members in effective ways. If its members provide it with more complete information about their activities, it could synthesize that information into a more accurate and relevant threat assessment than any member could produce on its own. It is always a challenge to secure multinational information sharing, as discussed in the next chapter, but if successful, synthesizing such information may reveal previously undetected patterns of terrorist movements across national borders and enable Europol to provide real-time actionable information to national authorities. As Europol develops increased capabilities in these areas, terrorists will find it increasingly difficult to take advantage of gaps in communication among European law enforcement agencies.

Strengthening Eurojust

In October 1999, the EU decided to establish a new organization, called Eurojust, to increase judicial cooperation among its members.[55] It became fully operational in February 2002, in accordance with the original timetable, but the September 11 attacks certainly reaffirmed the need for such an organization. It brings together prosecutors and magistrates from across the EU, enabling them to coordinate investigations, exchange information on criminal matters, and provide mutual legal assistance for cases that involve at least two EU member states. Eurojust also enables direct contact between judges, so that, for example, a judge in Greece can ask a judge in France to issue an order against a suspect living in France.[56]

Eurojust does not have the authority to launch or execute investigations, but instead relies on a system of lateral links among its members. Like Europol, Eurojust relies on the principle that the whole is greater than the sum of its parts, and that cross-border issues such as terrorism and organized crime require increased cooperation among judicial authorities.[57] Eurojust is a very young organization that is still establishing its own procedures and mechanisms for cooperation. But just as Europol may limit the ability of terrorists to hide in

---

[55]"Presidency Conclusions of the Tampere European Council," October 15 and 16, 1999, available at http://europa.eu.int/council/off/conclu/oct99/oct99_en.htm.

[56]Interviews with U.S. and EU officials, July 2002.

[57]Interviews with U.S. and EU officials, July 2002.

the gaps between European law enforcement agencies, Eurojust may also limit their ability to hide in the gaps between different legal jurisdictions by moving Europe one step closer to a single judicial area.

Combating Terrorist Financing

Starting in 1999, the European Union has adopted a number of measures designed to counter the financing of organized crime, including terrorism. The Conclusions of the Tampere European Council, held in October 1999, included crime-fighting proposals such as calling for a common definition of money laundering and increasing the transparency of financial transactions.[58] At the Council's request, the European Commission created what became known as the Scorecard, which tracks progress on enacting the Tampere Conclusions.[59] Another notable step forward occurred in September 2000 when the JHA Council extended Europol's competence to include all issues related to money laundering.[60] The following month, JHA held its first joint meeting with the Council of Economic and Finance Ministers (ECOFIN), where they discussed cooperative measures to increase their effectiveness in countering money laundering.

The September 11 attacks brought new urgency to this issue and generated the political will to break some of the political logjams that had been hindering further progress. The JHA Council held an emergency session on September 20, 2001, and its conclusions included an agreement to expedite measures (such as freezing of assets) to fight financial crimes related to terrorism and other transnational crimes, including money laundering.[61] The following day, the European Council adopted a plan to counter terrorism that included

---

[58]Other provisions called upon all EU members to adopt the recommendations of the Financial Action Task Force, expanding Europol's role in financial investigations, preventing offshore money laundering, and identifying legal inhibitions to money laundering. Occhipinti, pp. 83–85.

[59]Occhipinti, p. 86.

[60]Prior to this agreement, Europol was authorized to investigate money laundering only if it was related to one of the other crimes listed in its mandate. Occhipinti, p. 100.

[61]Occhipinti, pp. 150–151.

a commitment to pass EU legislation on money laundering and the freezing of terrorist assets.[62] JHA and ECOFIN held another joint meeting on October 16, 2001, where EU members overcame their previous disagreements and reached agreement on a more stringent directive regarding money laundering.[63] In December 2001, the European Parliament passed a legislative package that approved this directive and that ordered the freezing of assets belonging to the persons and groups listed in the annex to the Framework Decision on Combating Terrorism.[64]

Because it can set standards for its members in this important area, the EU is extremely well positioned to help efforts to combat terrorist financing. After the next round of enlargement in May 2004, the EU will expand from 15 to 25 members, ranging from the founding states of France and Germany to formerly communist countries such as Poland, Hungary, and the Baltic states.[65] All of them will be required to harmonize their positions on money laundering, asset freezing, and other actions to combat terrorist financing, which will make it much more difficult for terrorist individuals and groups to transfer funds through the European banking and financial sectors.

---

[62]The plan also called for the EU to sign and ratify the UN Convention for the Suppression of the Financing of Terrorism and action against noncooperative countries. Occhipinti, p. 152.

[63]Occhipinti, pp. 157–158.

[64]At the time, there were 29 individuals and 13 groups identified on the list. This measure was deliberately designed to be consistent with the provisions of UN Security Council Resolution 1373, adopted on September 28, 2001. Occhipinti, p. 179.

[65]The ten countries that will join the EU in 2004 are Cyprus, the Czech Republic, Estonia, Hungary, Latvia, Lithuania, Malta, Poland, Slovakia, and Slovenia.

Chapter Four

IMPLICATIONS FOR THE UNITED STATES

The European political environment comprises a complex set of national and international institutions. Individual countries retain primacy in certain areas while multinational institutions become increasingly powerful in others. As the United States develops a policy of counterterror cooperation with Europe, it must strike the right balance between bilateral and multilateral approaches. The policy choice is not *whether* to pursue a bilateral or multilateral strategy; so many important policies are now being made at the European level that multilateral institutions cannot simply be ignored. Instead, the United States must determine *which issues* are best addressed through a multilateral approach, and which ones are best addressed through a bilateral approach.

This chapter argues that the United States should pursue multilateral cooperation in the financial and law enforcement areas of counterterrorism, while pursuing military and intelligence cooperation on a bilateral basis.[1] The European Union has made extraordinary progress in Justice and Home Affairs in recent years, and although there is still a long way to go, the EU is uniquely positioned to coordinate its members' efforts, to analyze data, and to identify emerging trends throughout the continent. By contrast, the United States should pursue military and intelligence cooperation primarily on a bilateral basis with individual countries. European institutions are

---

[1]This distinction draws on the framework of multiple coalitions developed in a forthcoming RAND report by Nora Bensahel. Briefly stated, that framework asserts that there is not a single coalition against terrorism, but rather multiple coalitions in multiple issue areas, including the military, law enforcement, and intelligence.

either incapable (the EU) or unwilling (NATO) to serve a useful centralized role in these areas.

MULTILATERAL APPROACHES: FINANCIAL AND LEGAL COOPERATION

The United States should pursue an increasingly multilateral approach in its efforts to secure European financial and law enforcement cooperation, in which the EU has made remarkable progress in recent years. The European Union is unlikely to develop full supranational competence in these areas any time soon, but its efforts to promote closer cooperation will reduce the sometimes considerable legal and judicial discrepancies among its members and will enable law enforcement authorities to identify and track suspected terrorists through EU territory.

In the financial area, the EU has adopted a number of measures that are harmonizing the efforts of its members (and candidate members) in combating terrorist financing. These measures are helping to increase the transparency of financial transactions, to make money laundering more difficult, and to freeze the assets of groups and individuals that have been officially linked to terrorist activities. National attempts to combat terrorist financing remain important, but this is an inherently transnational problem, so that efforts at the EU level may ultimately be more effective than individual national efforts. At a minimum, each EU member will be following the same approach, thus preventing terrorists from taking advantage of gaps in national policies. Over time, the EU may become even more proactive in this area. It might, for example, serve as a central repository of information on suspicious financial transactions, and thus provide a more complete picture of terrorist activities than any individual state could provide on its own.

In the law enforcement area, the EU has significantly increased its collective crime-fighting capacity since 1999. It has expanded Europol and Eurojust and created an Operational Task Force of Police Chiefs and a European Police College.[2] Such measures will make it easier to identify, track, and prosecute suspected terrorists,

_____

[2]Occhipinti, pp. 3–4.

and it is hoped will help prevent future terrorist attacks. Furthermore, the EU will face continuing pressure to increase law enforcement cooperation as it expands to include countries from central and eastern Europe.[3] Although these pressures arise from concerns about organized crime and illegal immigration, measures to address these transnational issues will likely spill over and facilitate counterterror cooperation as well.

The EU has worked very hard to increase counterterror cooperation with the United States, particularly in law enforcement. Cooperation with Europol and Eurojust expanded considerably after September 11, especially when Europol invoked its risk-to-life clause and announced that it would share any information related to the attacks with the United States.[4] In December 2001, Europol signed a cooperation agreement with the United States that allows for sharing threat assessments and analysis, and it established a liaison office in Washington in August 2002. The United States has also exchanged liaison personnel with Eurojust and is starting to discuss signing an official agreement with that organization as well.[5] Some U.S. officials remain skeptical about the value of these liaison arrangements, because of continuing restrictions on information sharing and the difficulty of cooperating with the more than 30 U.S. federal law enforcement agencies.[6]

In the past, U.S.-EU police and judicial cooperation remained limited by disagreements over two important issues: personal data protection, and extradition and multilateral legal assistance. But the new political will generated by the September 11 attacks enabled both sides to reach acceptable compromises in both of these areas, which will significantly enhance their ability to cooperate in counterterrorism as well as other transnational issues.

---

[3]Occhipinti argues that the prospect of enlargement has been one of the most important external factors affecting the development of EU cooperation in the Justice and Home Affairs area since the late 1990s, and that it will continue to be so in the future.

[4]Europol officials, for example, helped U.S. authorities check European phone numbers called by the alleged hijackers. Occhipinti, p. 166.

[5]Dubois, p. 328; interviews with U.S. and EU officials, July 2002.

[6]Archick, p. CRS-12.

Personal Data Protection

The European Union and the United States have adopted different approaches to the problem of protecting personal information such as travel and communications records and the like. Many EU members feel strongly about this issue, given their historical experiences with fascism. The Europeans have enacted stringent laws—both at the national and at the EU level—that regulate the storage and sharing of personal information. By contrast, the United States protects personal information through legal precedents and procedures rather than legislation, arguing that safeguards cannot be provided through legislation in a federal system that incorporates more than 18,000 law enforcement jurisdictions. The Europeans have been concerned that the U.S. approach does not offer them enough safeguards to satisfy their legal requirements, and they have often refused to share personal information with the United States. This disagreement has posed real problems for counterterrorism cooperation, because personal data often provide the only evidence of connections between members of terrorist groups and the types of activities that they are conducting.[7]

The United States and the Europeans reached an acceptable compromise in December 2002, when the United States and Europol signed an agreement that allows for the exchange of personal data.[8] The agreement has made the U.S. relationship with Europol more operational by establishing principles for sharing specific information about individuals rather than just general trend data. A number of limitations remain, including the provision that personal information can be used only for the specific investigation for which it was requested. If, for example, information about a suspect in a murder case reveals links to money laundering, a supplemental request must be filed and approved before that information can be used in a money laundering case. Furthermore, the agreement applies only to law enforcement; it does not extend to the commercial area, where

---

[7]Interviews with U.S. and EU officials, July 2002.

[8]A draft of the agreement is available at http://register.consilium.eu.int/pdf/en/02/st15/15231en2.pdf.

disagreements remain about the proper safeguards for personal information.[9]

As of this writing, implementing the December 2002 agreement has been proceeding slowly. Procedures for information sharing are still being worked out, and, as discussed in Chapter 3, Europol's limited operational role restricts the amount of information available to be shared. Despite this slow implementation, the agreement has already had an important effect: it has established the principle of *adequacy*. Through this agreement, the Europeans have implicitly, if not explicitly, acknowledged that the U.S. system of protecting personal information adequately meets European standards, and that the system should no longer pose a barrier to information sharing among law enforcement officials. The agreement therefore establishes an important principle, and it enables the United States and Europol to develop patterns of cooperation that will become increasingly beneficial as Europol's operational role expands.[10]

Extradition and Mutual Legal Assistance

In the past, the United States and the EU members have also disagreed on a number of issues related to extradition and legal assistance. The death penalty has been a particularly controversial issue and has already hampered some investigations into the September 11 attacks.[11] Bilateral treaties with individual EU members have generally contained assurances that suspects extradited to the United States will not face the death penalty, but U.S. officials have been reluctant to agree to such a blanket guarantee in a treaty negotiated with the EU as a whole.[12]

At their May 2002 joint summit, both the United States and the EU agreed in principle to pursue a treaty on extradition and a mutual le-

---

[9]Interview with U.S. government official, April 2003.

[10]Interview with U.S. government official, April 2003.

[11]In September 2002, Germany told the United States that it would withhold evidence against Zacarias Moussaoui, who is charged with participating in the September 11 conspiracy, unless it received assurances that the death penalty would not be sought. See Kate Connolly, "Berlin Faces U.S. Fury Over 'Hijacker,'" *The Guardian* (London), September 2, 2002.

[12]Archick, p. CRS-14.

gal assistance treaty (MLAT). Such treaties would be the first of their kind, negotiated between the United States and the EU as an institutional actor. The United States held many meetings with representatives from Denmark, which held the rotating EU presidency between July and December 2002, and made much faster progress than either side had anticipated. By the end of the Danish presidency, they finalized the texts of both treaties. The treaties cover a wide range of issues, and the extradition treaty allows states to grant extradition on the condition that the death penalty will not be imposed.[13]

However, as of this writing neither treaty has been approved by the JHA Council. Some EU members oppose the treaties, calling into question whether they will be officially adopted. One stumbling block has to do with the priority assigned to U.S. requests for extradition and assistance. Initial drafts of the treaties contained language that would give extradition and assistance requests from EU member states a higher priority than requests from the United States and third parties. The Danish presidency removed these provisions, at the U.S. request. The agreed text therefore now states that if a country receives more than one extradition request for a specific person, that country can choose which request to honor.[14] Yet some EU members want EU requests to retain a higher priority than requests from third countries. It is not yet clear whether the EU members will be able to bridge their differences on this issue. Because the JHA Council must approve any treaties in this area by unanimous vote, any one state can prevent the treaties from entering into force.[15] Yet

---

[13]The draft also states that if procedural reasons prevent states from complying with this provision (as is often the case for U.S. prosecutors), states can grant extradition on the condition that the death penalty will not be carried out if it is imposed. The text of both draft treaties can be found at http://www.statewatch.org/news/2003/mar/document.pdf.

[14]The agreed text states that countries may consider many factors in making this decision, including "whether the requests were made pursuant to a treaty; the places where each of the offenses were committed; the respective interests of the requesting States; the gravity of the offenses; the nationality of the victim; the possibility of any subsequent extradition between the requesting States; and the chronological order in which the requests were received from requesting States." See Article 10 of the draft extradition treaty.

[15]For Justice and Home Affairs, the EU presidency possesses the authority to negotiate treaties, but they must be approved by the JHA Council. This complicated decision procedure results from the fact that JHA is the Third Pillar of the EU, which

the very fact that the United States and the EU presidency were able to reach agreement on the text so quickly is a promising sign, and even if the treaties do not enter into force, the negotiating process has revealed areas of common interest that can be further explored in future negotiations.

BILATERAL APPROACHES: MILITARY AND INTELLIGENCE COOPERATION

The United States should emphasize a bilateral approach in its efforts to secure European military and intelligence cooperation. Individual countries retain most of the relevant capabilities in these important areas, and European multilateral institutions have been incapable or unwilling to improve their capabilities. Although they may develop these capabilities over the long term, for the foreseeable future, effective counterterror cooperation in the military and intelligence fields will require focusing on bilateral approaches.

The EU has not made a significant contribution in the military and intelligence elements of the counterterrorism campaign because it possesses few institutional capacities in these areas. As discussed in Chapter Three, the EU lacks a single intelligence agency, which means that intelligence cooperation must occur on a bilateral basis. The European Security and Defense Policy remains at an early stage of development, and it is not designed to conduct the type of high-intensity, short-notice military actions that counterterrorism requires. As ESDP develops, it may become capable of conducting peacekeeping and reconstruction operations, which play an important role in preventing terrorists from taking root in ungoverned spaces.[16]   The EU is taking notable steps in this direction; for example, it has recently taken over peacekeeping

---

operates under the principle of intergovernmentalism and requires unanimous approval of all member states. The First Pillar (which includes a wide range of economic, social, and environmental issues) is the only one that operates under the principle of supranationalism, which gives the EU institutions the power to impose decisions on member states even if those states disagree. The three pillars were established as part of the 1992 Treaty on European Union (otherwise known as the Maastricht Treaty), which is available at http://europa.eu.int/en/record/mt/top.html.

[16]Bensahel will discuss the importance of reconstruction as an element of counterterrorism in a future report.

operations in Macedonia and is considering a similar role in Bosnia. The EU may be able to make a considerable military contribution here, but it is not planning to develop the type of capabilities necessary for offensive counterterror military operations.

The question of NATO's future role in counterterrorism is more complex. Many Europeans believed that the Article 5 invocation would lead to increased transatlantic cooperation against terrorism, but the United States decided to conduct Operation Enduring Freedom on a bilateral basis without any direct NATO role. The allies spent most of 2002 wrestling with the questions of why that occurred and what role NATO should play in future counterterror efforts. The Prague Summit endorsed some of the concepts that emerged from this debate, including the adoption of a new military concept against terrorism and a new capabilities initiative that will improve the alliance's ability to respond to short-notice crises. Yet the fundamental question about NATO's role in counterterrorism remains unanswered. Most of the allies believe that NATO needs to expand its authority and capabilities in this important area and must address related issues such as consequence management. Yet France has vocally challenged this position, arguing that NATO's role in counterterrorism is sufficient as it is now, and that related issues such as consequence management should be addressed through the European Union rather than NATO.

From a purely military perspective, September 11 showed that the United States does not need to draw on NATO to conduct military operations against suspected terrorists and their state sponsors. The United States demonstrated its ability to conduct a major offensive campaign in Afghanistan, along with smaller training operations in the Philippines, Georgia, and elsewhere, while limiting the NATO role to backfilling U.S. forces by patrolling U.S. airspace and the oceans off the Horn of Africa. To be sure, individual NATO allies did make significant military contributions, particularly in regard to special forces, but these were made on a bilateral basis and did not involve NATO's military staff. Barring a radical increase in European military capabilities—something which would take years to achieve, even under the best of circumstances—the United States will most likely choose to avoid giving NATO more than a minimal role in future military operations against terrorists and their sponsors. The United States should therefore emphasize bilateral military relationships when planning and conducting counterterror military operations, so that it can incorporate useful contributions from the willing without automatically involving all 19—and soon to be 26—alliance members in the decisionmaking process.

However, this does not mean that the United States should write off any NATO role in countering terrorism. The United States should encourage NATO to expand its counterterrorism efforts at the same time it pursues closer bilateral relations with individual allies, because NATO can make two unique contributions. First, NATO can provide diplomatic support for any counterterror operations conducted by its members. The Article 5 declaration was an important sign of political support for the United States, which helped establish the legitimacy of subsequent military operations in Afghanistan. The process of conducting threat assessments, identifying possible contingencies, and preparing operations plans will reinforce the principle that all of NATO's members share an interest in countering the common terrorism threat, which makes diplomatic support of any future counterterror operations more likely. Second, a continuing NATO focus on terrorism may encourage the European allies to increase their own preparations for counterterror activities, including homeland security and consequence management as well as military preparations. Although France wants the European Union to take responsibility for these sorts of issues, the United States has a strong interest in ensuring that the issues are addressed within NATO, where it has a voice at the table. That way, the United States can ensure that U.S. and European efforts remain coordinated, so that they complement each other instead of duplicating some efforts and overlooking others.

BALANCING BILATERAL AND MULTILATERAL POLICIES

Countering terrorism is an inherently challenging task requiring deep and sustained international cooperation across a wide range of issue areas. To date, the United States has chosen a strategy built primarily on bilateral relationships with the Europeans. The minimal role that NATO played in Operation Enduring Freedom demonstrates that even when a multilateral option exists, the United States often prefers to pursue counterterror cooperation through bilateral channels.

As European multilateral institutions continue to grow and evolve, however, a bilateral approach may no longer serve U.S. interests as effectively as it does now. This report argues that bilateral cooperation will likely remain necessary in military and intelligence counterterror cooperation, because NATO currently lacks the political will to embrace counterterrorism as a new mission and the EU does not intend to build the centralized structures and offensive military capabilities that would be required. However, multilateral cooperation will become increasingly important in financial and law enforcement cooperation as the EU continues to expand cooperation in Justice and Home Affairs. Many JHA initiatives are still in a relatively early stage of development, which means that the United States will still want to pursue bilateral cooperation with individual states to secure the information it needs for the counterterror campaign. Yet JHA cooperation has proceeded remarkably quickly since it began in 1999, and as it continues to develop, the United States will have to adopt an increasingly multilateral approach to keep pace with these developments. Strengthened JHA cooperation is in the best interest of the United States as well as the European Union, because it will help generate a more complete picture of the terrorist threat. Multilateral cooperation with an increasingly strong European Union will enhance the ability of states on both sides of the Atlantic to prevent terrorism and to prosecute those involved in terrorist activities.

EUROPEAN AND CANADIAN CONTRIBUTIONS TO OPERATION ENDURING FREEDOM, OCTOBER 2001– OCTOBER 2002[1]

This appendix lists forces that were made available for combat operations as part of Operation Enduring Freedom; it does not include humanitarian assistance or contributions to the International Security Assistance Force (ISAF).

Albania

Basing and access rights
- Seaport refueling and maintenance

Overflight rights
- Granted to NATO aircraft involved in OEF

Bulgaria

Basing and access rights

Overflight rights

---

[1] SOURCES: Department of Defense Public Affairs Fact Sheet, *International Contributions to the War Against Terrorism*, June 7, 2002 (Revised June 14, 2002); U.S. Central Command, "International Contributions to the War on Terrorism," available through http://www.centcom.mil/Operations/Coalition/joint.htm, accessed November 2002; The White House, "Campaign Against Terrorism: An Update," issued March 11, 2002, available at http://www.whitehouse.gov/march11/campaignagainst terrorism.pdf; and information provided by individual embassies.

Canada

Air forces
- One CC-150 Polaris aircraft and three CC-130 Hercules aircraft, conducting strategic and tactical airlift

Ground forces
- A Light Infantry Battle Group, composed primarily of forces from the 3rd Battalion, Princess Patricia's Canadian Light Infantry, including 830 personnel and 12 armored reconnaissance vehicles

Naval forces
- A naval task group, which at its peak included six warships and 1500 personnel

- Two CP-140 Aurora (P-3C) patrol and surveillance aircraft, with 200 personnel

- Helicopter assets

Special operations forces

Czech Republic

Basing and access rights
- Provided to U.S. and coalition forces

Overflight rights
- Provided to U.S. and coalition forces

Other forces
- The 9th Fortified Radiation, Chemical, and Biological Protection Company, with 251 personnel

Denmark

Air forces
- One C-130 aircraft

- Six F-16 aircraft

Special operations forces

Estonia

Basing and access rights
- Provided to U.S. and coalition partners

Overflight rights
- Provided to U.S. and coalition partners

Other forces
- An explosives detection dog team, with five specialists and three dogs

France

Air forces
- Six Mirage 2000 fighter aircraft, conducting close air support missions from Manas

- Two C-135-FR refueling aircraft, providing aerial refueling from Manas

- Two Mirage IV P-Recce and two C-160s, for strategic reconnaissance and intelligence gathering

- C-160 and C-130 aircraft, providing airlift support

- Two MPA Atlantique 2 aircraft, conducting maritime surveillance from Djibouti

Basing and access rights

Ground forces
- An infantry company deployed to Mazar-e-Sharif, to provide area security through December 2001

Naval forces
- The *Charles de Gaulle* aircraft carrier and its battle group, supporting combat operations in the North Arabian Sea with air reconnaissance, strike, and airborne early warning (AEW) missions

- One oiler

- One nuclear attack submarine

- Two frigates
- A maritime intelligence task group, with five ships
- A minesweeping task group, with three ships

Overflight rights

Special operations forces

Germany

Air forces
- Six C-130 aircraft

Naval forces
- Three frigates, one fast patrol boat group, and four supply ships operating in the Gulf of Aden, based in Djibouti
- Two Sea King helicopters, based in Djibouti
- Three maritime patrol aircraft, based in Kenya

Special operations forces

Other forces
- One nuclear, biological, and chemical unit
- One medical evacuation A-310 aircraft

Greece

Basing and access rights
- The Greek naval base and air base of Souda, Crete, and other bases used as forward logistics sites for ships in the region

Ground forces
- An engineering unit

Naval forces
- One frigate with a special forces team and a helicopter

Hungary

Overflight rights

Italy

Air forces
- One C-130 and one Boeing 707, based in Manas

- An engineer team, which repaired the runway at Bagram

Naval forces
- A carrier battle group operating in the North Arabian Sea, replaced by the *Durand De La Penne* group including a destroyer and a frigate, and then replaced by the frigate *Euro*

Latvia

Air forces
- One air movement control team, deployed with a Danish contingent

Basing and access rights

Overflight rights

Lithuania

Basing and access rights

Overflight rights

The Netherlands

Air forces
- Six F-16s, for reconnaissance

- One KDC-10 tanker

- One C-130 transport airplane

Naval forces
- Four maritime patrol airplanes

- Three frigates

- Two minesweepers

- One submarine

Norway

Air forces
- C-130 aircraft, providing tactical airlift support, national resupply missions, and humanitarian assistance missions
- Six F-16s deployed to Manas

Special operations forces

Other forces
- Hydrema-910 mine-clearing vehicles, operating in and around Kandahar and Bagram airfields

Poland

Basing and access rights
- Provided for U.S. and coalition forces

Naval forces
- A logistics support ship scheduled to deploy to the region

Overflight rights
- Provided for U.S. and coalition forces

Special operations forces

Other forces
- Combat engineers and logistics forces

Portugal

Air forces
- One C-130 transport aircraft, with 15 personnel

Other forces
- One eight-person medical team

Romania

Basing and access rights
- Provided for U.S. and coalition forces

Ground forces
- 405 troops from the 26th Infantry Battalion

- A motorized infantry battalion

Overflight rights
- Provided for U.S. and coalition forces

Russia

Other capabilities
- A hospital provided in Kabul, turned over to the local population in January 2002

Slovakia

Basing and access rights
- Provided for U.S. and coalition forces

Overflight rights
- Provided for U.S. and coalition forces

Other forces
- A 40-person engineering unit

Spain

Air forces
- Two C-130s deployed to Manas

Basing and access rights
- Standard clearance authority for landing at air bases

Naval forces
- Two naval frigates

- One supply ship

- One P-3B maritime patrol aircraft, operating from Djibouti

- Two search and rescue helicopters, operating from Manas

Overflight rights

Other capabilities
*   A hospital in Bagram

Turkey

Air forces
*   KC-135 aerial refueling support

Basing and access rights
*   Provided for U.S. and coalition forces

Ground forces
*   One infantry unit

Overflight rights
*   Provided for U.S. and coalition forces

Special operations forces

Ukraine

Basing and access rights
*   Offered U.S. forces access to three air bases

Overflight rights
*   Provided for U.S. and coalition forces

United Kingdom

Air forces
*   Tristars aerial tankers

*   E-3D Sentry AWACS

*   Nimrod R1 surveillance aircraft

*   Canberra PR-9 reconnaissance aircraft

Basing and access
*   Granted access to Diego Garcia

Ground forces
*   A 1700-person infantry battle group, built around 45-Commando, Royal Marines, operating as part of a U.S.-led brigade

Naval forces
- Submarines, including HMS *Superb*, HMS *Trafalgar*, and HMS *Triumph*

- The aircraft carrier HMS *Illustrious* and the assault ship HMS *Fearless*

- An Amphibious Task Group, including the HMS *Ocean*, the destroyer HMS *York*, the frigates HMS *Campbeltown* and HMS *Portland*, the survey ship HMS *Scott*, six ships from the Royal Fleet Auxiliary, and helicopters

- Nimrod MR2 maritime patrol aircraft

Special operations forces

Other forces
- A company from 40-Commando, Royal Marines, to assist with mine-clearing operations

BIBLIOGRAPHY

"190 French Troops Arrive in Kyrgyzstan to Help with Base," *Los Angeles Times*, February 3, 2002.

Archick, Kristin, *Europe and Counterterrorism: Strengthening Police and Judicial Cooperation*, Congressional Research Service Report to Congress, July 23, 2002.

Aznar, Jose Maria, et al., "European Leaders in Support of U.S.," *Wall Street Journal*, January 30, 2003.

Baker, Peter, "British Forces Lead New Afghan Mission," *Washington Post*, April 17, 2002.

Bowden, Mark, "The Kabul-ki Dance," *The Atlantic Monthly*, November 2002, pp. 66–87.

Brown, David, "Coalition Aircraft Patrol the Seas for Enduring Freedom," *Navy Times*, August 12, 2002.

Carassava, Anthee, "European Union and NATO Sign Pact," *New York Times*, March 15, 2003.

Champion, Marc, "Eight European Leaders Voice Their Support for U.S. on Iraq," *Wall Street Journal*, January 30, 2003.

Clark, Wesley, *Waging Modern War*, PublicAffairs, New York, 2001.

Colombani, Jean-Marie, "Nous sommes tous Américains," *Le Monde*, September 12, 2001.

"Conclusions and Plan of Action of the Extraordinary European Council Meeting on 21 September 2001," Press Release SN 140/01, September 21, 2001.

Connolly, Kate, "Berlin Faces U.S. Fury Over 'Hijacker,'" *The Guardian* (London), September 2, 2002.

"Council Framework Decision of June 13 2002 on Combating Terrorism," 2002/475/JHA.

Daalder, Ivo H., and Philip R. Gordon, "Euro-Trashing," *Washington Post*, May 29, 2002.

Daalder, Ivo H., and Michael E. O'Hanlon, *Winning Ugly: NATO's War to Save Kosovo*, Brookings Institution Press, Washington, D.C., 2000.

Daley, Suzanne, "For First Time, NATO Invokes Pact with U.S.," *New York Times*, September 13, 2001.

"Decision Adopted by Written Procedure: Fight Against Terrorism—Updated List," 8549/02 (Presse 121), Brussels, May 3, 2002.

Den Boer, Monica, and Jörg Monar, "Keynote Article: 11 September and the Challenge of Global Terrorism to the EU as a Security Actor," *Journal of Common Market Studies*, Vol. 40, Annual Review, 2002, pp. 11–28.

Department of Defense Public Affairs Fact Sheet, *International Contributions to the War Against Terrorism*, June 7, 2002 (revised June 14, 2002).

DeYoung, Karen, "For Powell, a Long Path to a Victory," *Washington Post*, November 10, 2002.

DeYoung, Karen, and Colum Lynch, "Three Countries Vow to Block U.S. on Iraq," *Washington Post*, March 6, 2003.

Dobbs, Michael, "Waylaid at Sea: Launch of Policy; Handling of Scuds Raises Questions," *Washington Post*, December 13, 2002.

Dorsey, Jack, "NATO Air Surveillance Help Makes American Skies Safer," *Norfolk Virginian-Pilot*, October 24, 2001.

Dubois, Dorine, "The Attacks of 11 September: EU-US Cooperation Against Terrorism in the Field of Justice and Home Affairs," *European Foreign Policy Review*, Vol. 7, 2002, pp. 317–335.

Embassy of France in the United States, "French Military Contibution [sic] to the Fight Against Terrorism," available at http://www.ambafrance-us.org/news/statmnts/2002/sfia/fight1. asp, accessed October 4, 2002.

Erlanger, Steven, "Rumsfeld Urges NATO to Set Up Strike Force," *New York Times*, September 25, 2002.

Evans, Michael, "SAS Already Gathering Intelligence in Afghanistan," *The Times* (London), September 21, 2001.

_____, "Royal Marines Heading for Risky Task of Ferreting Out Bin Laden," *The Times* (London), October 26, 2001.

Fact Sheet, "NATO: Building New Capabilities for New Challenges," The White House, Office of the Press Secretary, November 21, 2002.

"Final Communiqué: Ministerial Meeting of the North Atlantic Council Held in Reykjavik on 14 May 2002," Press Release M-NAC-1(2002)59, May 14, 2002.

Finn, Peter, "U.S.-Europe Rifts Widen Over Iraq," *Washington Post*, February 11, 2003.

Fiorenza, Nicholas, "Alliance Solidarity," *Armed Forces Journal International*, December 2001, p. 22.

_____, "NATO to Adopt Capabilities Plan," *Defense News*, November 18–24, 2002.

Fitchett, Joseph, "NATO Unity, But What Next?" *International Herald Tribune*, September 14, 2001.

_____, "Pentagon in a League of Its Own," *International Herald Tribune*, February 4, 2002.

_____, "NATO Agrees to Help New EU Force," *International Herald Tribune*, December 16, 2002.

Gordon, Michael R., "NATO Chief Says Alliance Needs Role in Afghanistan," *New York Times*, February 21, 2003.

Gordon, Philip H., "NATO After 11 September," *Survival*, Vol. 43, No. 4, Winter 2001–2002, pp. 89–106.

Graham, Bradley, and Robert G. Kaiser, "NATO Ministers Back U.S. Plan for Rapid Reaction Force," *Washington Post*, September 25, 2002.

Hoge, Warren, "British Official Says Troops for Afghanistan Are Off High Alert," *New York Times*, November 27, 2001.

Hunter, Robert E., *The European Security and Defense Policy: NATO's Companion—or Competitor?* RAND, MR-1463-NDRI/RE, 2002.

Kaminski, Matthew, "NATO's Low Priority on Terrorism Leaves It Ill Prepared for Latest War," *Wall Street Journal*, October 5, 2001.

Kitfield, James, "NATO Metamorphosis," *National Journal*, Vol. 34, No. 6, February 9, 2002.

"Laeken European Council: Extradition will no longer be necessary between EU member states," December 14–15, 2001, available at http://europa.eu.int/comm/justice_home/news/laeken_council/en/mandat_en.htm.

Lansford, Tom, *All for One: Terrorism, NATO and the United States*, Ashgate, Aldershot, UK, 2002.

Lewis, J. A. C., "French Fighters Join Action in Afghanistan," *Jane's Defence Weekly*, March 13, 2002.

McNeil, Jr., Donald J., "Europe Moves to Toughen Laws to Fight Terrorism," *New York Times*, September 20, 2001.

Mediterranean Dialogue Work Programme, available at http://www.nato.int/med-dial/2002/mdwp-2002.pdf.

Muradian, Vago, "NATO Remains Key, But U.S. Ready to Fight Antiterror War Without Europe," *Defense Daily International*, February 8, 2002.

"NATO's Response to Terrorism: Statement issued at the ministerial meeting of the North Atlantic Council held at NATO Headquarters, Brussels, on 6 December 2001," Press Release M-NAC-2(2001)159, December 6, 2001.

Naumann, Klaus, "How to Close the Capabilities Gap," *Wall Street Journal*, May 23, 2002.

"New Allies Back U.S. Iraq Policy," *International Herald Tribune*, February 6, 2003.

Occhipinti, John D., *The Politics of EU Police Cooperation*, Lynne Rienner Publishers, Boulder, CO, 2003.

"Operation Veritas—British Forces," British Ministry of Defence, available at http://www.operations.mod.uk/veritas/forces.htm.

Peters, John E., Stuart Johnson, Nora Bensahel, Timothy Liston, and Traci Williams, *European Contributions to Operation Allied Force*, RAND, MR-1391-AF, 2001.

Piatt, Gregory, "NATO's AWACS Leaving Skies Over U.S., Returning to Europe," *Baltimore Sun*, April 25, 2002.

Prague Summit Declaration, NATO Press Release (2002)127, November 21, 2002.

"Presidency Conclusions of the Tampere European Council," October 15 and 16, 1999, available at http://europa.eu.int/council/off/conclu/oct99/oct99_en.htm.

Preston, Julia, "France Warns U.S. It Will Not Back Early War on Iraq," *New York Times*, January 21, 2003.

"Proposal for a Council Framework Decision on Combating Terrorism," COM(2001) 521 final, Brussels, September 19, 2001.

Reid, T. R., "Britain Set to Bulk Up Its Afghan Deployment," *Washington Post*, March 19, 2002.

Rice, Condoleezza, "Our Coalition," *Wall Street Journal*, March 26, 2003.

Richburg, Keith B., "Key Allies Not Won Over By Powell," *Washington Post*, February 7, 2003.

Ricks, Thomas E., and Peter Slevin, "Spain and U.S. Seize N. Korean Missiles," *Washington Post*, December 11, 2002.

Savic, Misha, "EU Peacekeepers Arrive in Macedonia," *Washington Post*, April 1, 2003.

Schmitt, Eric, "NATO Planes to End Patrols of U.S. Skies," *New York Times*, May 2, 2002.

"Secretary Rumsfeld Briefs at the Foreign Press Center," January 22, 2003, available at http://www.defenselink.mil/news/Jan2003/t01232003_t0122sdfpc.html.

Shapiro, Jeremy, *The Role of France in the War on Terrorism*, Center on the United States and France, Brookings Institution, May 2002.

Shishkin, Philip, "Europe Must Strengthen Military, Say Concerned Defense Officials," *Wall Street Journal*, February 4, 2002.

_____, "Robertson, NATO's Head, Seeks to Fix Credibility," *Wall Street Journal*, February 19, 2003.

_____, "Europe Has Chance to Prove Mettle in Current Offensive in Afghanistan," *Wall Street Journal*, March 6, 2002.

_____, "European NATO Leaders Say War Planning Undermines U.N.," *Wall Street Journal*, January 21, 2003.

Smith, Craig S., with Richard Bernstein, "3 NATO Members and Russia Resist U.S. on Iraq Plans," *New York Times*, February 11, 2003.

Smith, Michael, "Hoon Confirms that British Troops Are on the Front Line," *The Daily Telegraph* (London), November 12, 2001.

"Statement by the North Atlantic Council," Press Release PR/CP (2001)122, September 11, 2001.

"Statement by the North Atlantic Council," Press Release (2001)124, September 12, 2001.

"Statement by NATO Secretary General, Lord Robertson," October 2, 2001.

"Statement to the Press by NATO Secretary General, Lord Robertson, on the North Atlantic Council Decision on Implementation of Article 5 of the Washington Treaty Following the 11 September Attacks Against the United States," October 4, 2001.

"Statement by NATO Secretary General, Lord Robertson," Press Release (2001)138, October 8, 2001.

U.S. Central Command, "International Contributions to the War on Terrorism," available at http://www.centcom.mil/Operations/Coalition/joint.htm, accessed November 2002.

Weisman, Steven R., "A Long, Winding Road to a Diplomatic Dead End," *New York Times*, March 17, 2003.

Yost, David S., "The NATO Capabilities Gap and the European Union," *Survival*, Vol. 42, No. 4, Winter 2000–2001, pp. 97–128.